COPPER
LADY

Jenny Otten

COPPER LADY

LIFE IN THE MET AND LORDS

BARONESS JENNY HILTON

AMBERLEY

First published 2020

Amberley Publishing
The Hill, Stroud
Gloucestershire, GL5 4EP

www.amberley-books.com

ISBN 978 1 3981 0780 9 (hardback)
ISBN 978 1 3981 0781 6 (ebook)

British Library Cataloguing in Publication Data.
A catalogue record for this book is available
from the British Library.

1 2 3 4 5 6 7 8 9 10

Typesetting by Aura Technology and Software
Services, India. Printed in the UK.

CONTENTS

Prologue 7

1 Cyprus and Bristol 9

2 Wartime 16

3 Greece 26

4 Bedales 37

5 Paris 52

6 Bethnal Green 61

7 Istanbul 68

8 Recruit 73

9 Stepney 77

10 Kings Cross 91

11 Turkish Interregnum 99

12 Promotion 104

13 Inspector 117

14 Manchester University 123

15 Return to the Met 130

16 Police Staff College 137

17 Management Services 144

18 Airport Division 147

19 Battersea 153

20 Senior Command Course and Chiswick 160

21 Planning Group   170

22 Commander   174

23 Hendon   182

24 Retirement   189

25 House of Lords   194

Appendices

1 Origins   207

2 My Father's Family Tree   216

3 My Mother's Family Tree   217

4 Speech on Iraq 2002   218

5 Speech on International Affairs 2019   221

PROLOGUE

I originally intended this to be a memoir only about my time in the police service and about how I ended up in the House of Lords. I was motivated to write because of a discussion with two friends about the television series *Call the Midwife*. When I said, 'Of course, I was a police officer at the other end of Stepney at that time,' my friend Victoria said, 'Well, you should write about it.'

However, as I began writing about my time in the police service I realised that I needed to explain how, coming from an artistic and professional family, I took up an occupation that my great-aunt Saintie described as 'not quite out of the top drawer, dear' and which a young man on the Paris Metro in 1955 described as a 'bizarre' idea, much to my irritation.

I had spectacularly failed all my A Levels at Bedales in the summer of 1954, and as all my school friends went off to university I looked for work as something other than a nurse or a secretary – which in 1954 were the main jobs for girls without qualifications.

Also, my mother and father were about to leave England for a four-year posting to Turkey with the Foreign Office, so I would be homeless. Crucially, the police service provided accommodation for its officers.

This memoir is therefore an attempt to explain how I came to my decision to join the Metropolitan Police.

I

CYPRUS AND BRISTOL

I was born in Cyprus on 12 January 1936. My parents came from middle-class, artistic and liberal backgrounds. My great-great-uncle Charles Harrison Townsend was a distinguished Arts and Crafts architect, responsible for the Horniman Museum, the Bishopsgate Institute and the Whitechapel Art Gallery, which were built in furtherance of William Morris's socialist ideals. My paternal great-grandmother, Suzette Hildesheim (née Warburg), was the sister of the founder of the Warburg Institute. Both my grandmothers studied at the Slade School of Art, as did my father's brother, Roger, who became a well-known abstract expressionist.

My mother had studied as an artist at the Slade and at Roger Bissière's studio in Paris. My father trained as an architect after Oxford. The 1930s were lean times for architects, however, and so in 1934 he had applied for a post as Director of Antiquities in Cyprus. The members of the Cyprus Committee were concerned about the state of disrepair of many of the island's historic buildings – a roof had just collapsed in Bellapais Abbey and St Hilarion Castle (the honeymoon location of Richard I and

Berengaria of Navarre) was crumbling – so they wanted an architect to oversee repairs. Unfortunately, although appointed by the Cyprus Committee, my father became an employee of the Colonial Office and was on probation for the first two years of what was intended to be a thirty-year appointment.

My naïve, artistic parents were not suited to the Colonial set-up, which was all white gloves and formal garden parties. Most of the friends they made were Cypriots – Porphyrios Dikaios, an expert on Neolithic Cyprus, whom I met many years later on a holiday in Cyprus, had been my father's deputy and later became head of the Cyprus Museum, and the delightful Diamantises, husband and wife, remained lifelong friends. There was also a rather shady man, Mogabgab (such an unforgettable name!), of Syrian origin, who ostracized my parents when they seemed to be in disgrace but was eager to re-establish the relationship many years later when my father was in the Foreign Office.

To begin with, in 1934 and 1935, all went well – they had a beautiful house with shady balconies surrounding a mature tree-filled garden and my father, with a gang of convicts for labour, enthusiastically began to protect Cyprus's decaying historic monuments. With the refectory roof in Bellapais Abbey having recently collapsed, he shored up the surviving chapel roof with telegraph poles. This was seen as a desecration by some who preferred crumbling ruins; it was a particular problem for the Deputy Governor, a man called Gunnis, who was allegedly in a homosexual relationship with the Governor. Gunnis was also conducting a thriving trade in smuggled antiques with the help of the village policemen, who alerted him to any fresh archaeological finds. Moreover, he was apparently (according to my father's sister Judy, my godmother) very charming to visiting English 'ladies', whom he accompanied on sightseeing tours around the island.

My naïve parents were not aware of this serpent in what my father certainly saw as an earthly paradise, and matters were made worse by my mother failing to wear white gloves to official garden parties and my father allegedly being too kind to his convict labourers, allowing them cups of tea. According to my mother, it is also possible that my father damaged his standing by rejecting Gunnis' sexual advances. Less than a year after his appointment, my father was summonsed on the long drive to see the British Colonial Governor at his summer residence in the cool heights of the central Troodos Mountains, where, shockingly, he was told he was being summarily dismissed without explanation. This was permissible, as he was within his two-year period of probation. (His father, Oscar, subsequently mounted a successful campaign to establish that there had been absolutely no reason for the dismissal and that my father had not transgressed in any way.)

My parents were allowed to stay for a few months as my mother was pregnant (with me), and so they left the lovely island when I was three months old, in April 1936. I think that my father's apparent failure, which he perceived as a tragedy, was a blow from which he never quite recovered. His mother's first-born son, he had always previously been very successful at school, obtaining a First in Politics, Philosophy and Economics at Oxford and winning prizes at the Royal Institute of British Architects. He subsequently wrote several sad, unpublished accounts of his time in Cyprus, describing the island as a sunlit, bee-loud land of endless delight.

I think my mother was less enthusiastic about the island, missing her family and friends and lacking any support during her pregnancy. Travel to Cyprus was more difficult in those days as it involved taking a boat from Marseille or Venice. There were, however, several visitors including my father's parents and sister and my godfather, Moore Crosthwaite (one of my father's gay friends, and later HM Ambassador to Lebanon). According to my aunt Judy, Crosthwaite sunbathed with his fingers spread out so as to tan the skin between!

I have since paid two visits to Cyprus. In 1959 I went on a month-long visit to my parents in Istanbul, and we went on a great camping expedition across Turkey by car, and then spent a week in Cyprus, where, despite the lapse of more than twenty years, they were well remembered. In 1968 I had a more ordinary holiday there with my sister Dinah, although I was also acting as a surrogate for my father, who was responsible for the probate of the will of one of his former secretaries who had settled there, and I had to meet with local lawyers and the town mayor. As a reward for this service, my father gave me a little prehistoric cup to add to my other relics from the island – a small idol (now donated to the British Museum), two eighth-century BC milk bowls and a marriage chest of carved cedar. Dinah and I stayed in lovely Kyrenia and revisited some buildings my father had helped preserve, including Bellapais Abbey and St Hilarion Castle. I drove us about in a hired car and became extremely irritated with Dinah, who did nothing but complain about the heat whilst I was doing all the work! It was extremely hot, and cows lay sleeping in the shade of the carob trees.

On my return to England I went to renew my passport and was told that I was entitled to Cypriot citizenship (birth and a recent visit being the qualifications) but would have to produce my parents' and grandparents' birth certificates if I wanted a British passport. My grandfather's change of name from Hildesheim to

Hilton (his family were German-Jewish jute merchants based in Dundee) during the First World War created particular difficulties for the authorities, so I had to produce a copy of the original deed poll. My father spent the first six years of his life as John Hildesheim and was half-Jewish. He hated the name change.

On my parents' return to England from Cyprus we went to live in a tall house in the Clifton area of Bristol, where my father had a job in the design department of a local firm. My mother's aunt Helen lived in Bristol at the time with her husband, Samuel Barnet (known as Uncle Uly – for many years I hoped this was short for Ulysses), and they helped my father find a job. He also designed a house in the art deco style and had it built for my maternal grandmother near Wallingford in Berkshire, where we were subsequently to find refuge from the heavy bombing raids on Bristol during the Second World War.

I was always climbing trees as a child, and my first conscious memory is of falling out of a bush in the public garden opposite our house in one of the Clifton terraces and being winded – a frightening experience. I had two brown-and-white mice as pets, but inevitably they escaped from their cage and went to live under the gas fire. In the bathroom, the bath was heated by a terrifying cylindrical geyser that hissed and rumbled. On one occasion, when I was about four, I walked in to find my father lying naked in the bath – embarrassed, he hurriedly covered himself with a sponge. I also remember sliding on the polished rocks on the Clifton Downs, and visits to the zoo to see the gorilla and to feed peanuts to the monkeys. I briefly went to a kindergarten where a boy tried to get me to eat cakes made out of wet sand. I also went to the infants' class of Clifton High School when I was four or five, and was puzzled by a teacher pointing at large panorama of sea and sand, saying in a significant voice, 'As idle as a painted ship upon a painted ocean.' Being ignorant of Coleridge's poem, this seemed to me rather obvious!

In September 1938, when my sister Dinah was born, I was taken by my paternal grandmother (Granny) and her sister Lilah for a holiday in Paignton, where I fell in love with a large starfish washed up on the beach. Early in the war, before bombs began to fall seriously on the Bristol Docks, my mother gave me a banana, saying, 'It's the last one until after the war.' There were barrage balloons like large sleepy elephants on the Bristol Downs, and when the air raid sirens went off we went down to the basement where our tenants lived and their teenage boy chased me round the table singing, 'Run rabbit run, the farmer's got his gun.' My father did fire-watching for a time and then enlisted in the Royal Engineers, where he became a Captain and built Bailey bridges. Although he was given embarkation leave (preparatory to being sent to a war zone) on several occasions, he was soon transferred to Military Intelligence and so to MI6, which accounts for his subsequent career in the Foreign Office and postings to Greece and Turkey.

He was away a lot during the war, and I idolized him – trying to imitate his illegible handwriting and knack for wordplay. In later life I often had to explain his elaborate puns to my mother, who as an artist thought in images rather than verbally and so never mastered crosswords but was an excellent card player. This failure to communicate was a source of low-level squabbles between them, which as a child I found painfully frightening, especially as my father could be very squashing, which my sister Dinah found particularly difficult. If I did not know something and asked for an explanation he was inclined to say, 'Everyone knows that!' and not bother to explain, so I was left feeling hurt and humiliated. My mother, in contrast, was always very enthusiastic and encouraging. When I was very small I had a doll called Baby Batty (I have her still), and when I did not know the answer to a question I would say, 'Baby Batty has a book about it.' I learnt to cope better later in life and had lively arguments with my father where we both consulted dictionaries and encyclopaedias to prove a point (Google would have been a godsend). He was often more physically demonstrative than my mother, given to sudden little affectionate hugs.

2

WARTIME

At the start of the war, we went for a time to stay in Berkshire with my maternal grandmother. We soon returned to Bristol, but in 1941, as the air raids on the docks worsened, we went to live there and remained until 1944.

My mother's mother, 'Pau-pau', Pauline Boucher, had been widowed for the second time when she was in her forties. She lived in a large, pink brick house with white trimmings in a broadly art deco style, which my father had designed. It was a mile outside Wallingford in Berkshire, halfway between Reading and Oxford. She and her unmarried sister, Aunt Saintie (St Clair Townsend), had bought three acres in the corner of a farmer's field on which they built houses. Aunt Saintie's was a long, low, wooden bungalow in silvery grey wood which was chewed by wasps for their nests each summer. It was called Grimms Dyke Cottage after the ancient British trackway which was a few hundred yards away across a field. She had one acre of garden in which she grew wonderful irises, rhubarb and sea-kale. During the war she also had two beehives and a succession of small dogs, mostly Pekingese.

There was a rockery and a row of lavender bushes dividing the garden from the rough grass below, which was studded with the bright blue of chicory flowers.

Pau-pau's two acres, in contrast, consisted mostly of rough pasture where we kept chickens – the eggs were preserved in a bucket of something called 'isinglass' – and there was a vegetable bed maintained by the gardener, Collett, who was with us until well into the war and was also responsible for stoking the furnaces in both houses. By the drive there were several Lombardy poplar trees languishing unhappily in the shallow, chalky soil. Pau-pau's house was called 'Crowsnest' because it was at the top of a hill with wonderful views westward to sunsets over the Oxford plain, with the Wittenham Clumps and the towers of Didcot Power Station in the far distance. There was no electricity, so we lived by candlelight and hissing oil lamps which had to be pumped by hand until the element glowed white hot. We did, however, have central heating, fed by the boiler in the dedicated boiler room. Water that came deliciously straight off the chalk of the Chilterns, with a special tap for drinking, had to be 'softened' by a complicated machine before it would produce a lather and could be used for washing. Sewage went into a cesspit far down the garden.

Now that I was five years old, my memories become clearer and more detailed. For a short time on our first visit (when I was four) I attended the village school in Wallingford, and I can only remember that the other older children teased me because I couldn't read silently to myself. When we went back to Berkshire in 1941 I went to Homer School, which was in woods above Henley in the last gasp of the Chiltern Hills. It had several acres of open space where we could roll enormous snowballs (it must have been that year that my father, home from the war, made an igloo) and build an ancient hut in the woods. On one occasion we were filmed picking foxglove leaves for digitalis as part of a propaganda film showing the contribution of schoolchildren to the war effort! Apart from being praised for learning my six times table and being criticised for being the untidiest girl in the school, I remember little about formal lessons, but I do remember the wartime puddings of sago, semolina and tapioca (frogspawn). On special occasions like Christmas parties we had jelly and dreadful pink blancmange and at home there was junket. I have never been a great enthusiast for puddings since.

I do remember being bitten by a mouse that I rescued from a cat and being in serious trouble for hitting another girl with the sheath knife (in its sheath) I had been given for Christmas. I always seemed to be given knives for Christmas so that I could make bows and arrows and play at being Robin Hood, wearing the green silk stockings from the dressing-up box. I always dressed as a boy. This was the first and last time I hit anybody, apart from on one occasion when I smacked Tom, my younger brother, when I was left in charge of him and he would not put on his cap for school.

Another first and last at the age of six was when I fell in love with a boy. He was called Christopher and had bright blonde hair. Curiously, at this stage of the war (spring 1942?) we had a holiday in Roseland, a promontory on the south coast of Cornwall, in a hotel perched on a cliff above a private cove. My father had undergone an appendectomy and this was part of his convalescence, although I do not remember him being there much. My grandmother, Pau-pau, was there for some of the time and told me off for letting a wave run over my shoes. There was another man there (perhaps a friend or an uncle) who introduced me to wonderful rock pools with fluorescent multihued seaweeds, hermit crabs and something called a sea lemon which looked like a yellow slug and was apparently an exciting find. It cannot have been summer because we did not paddle or swim, but there were cowrie shells to be found on the beach and my mother held a grass snake which she had found in the hotel garden. At the end of the holiday I filled an elegant glass bottle with shells, brightly coloured seaweeds and sea water and gave it to Christopher on my return to school. I do not recall that he was particularly pleased by the gift, and my passion for him died.

Towards the end of my time at Homer School I stayed overnight. My sister Dinah was only there for mornings, and my mother could not manage both of us on the back of her moped and could not do more than one journey a day due to petrol rationing – even though it was only a few miles each way. I understood this but felt very bereft (and jealous?) when I saw my mother leave with my sister on the pillion. It was no recompense that one of the teachers kissed me goodnight with 'butterfly' kisses.

One important feature of living with my grandmother and next door to my great-aunt was the obligatory after-lunch half-hour rest and then a walk whatever the weather. 'Exercise is good for you,' they said. Although they had been brought up in Canada and were made nostalgic by seeing drifts of rosebay willow herb ('fireweed' as they called it) in the woods, they were enthusiastic gardeners and amateur botanists and taught me the lovely names of the chalkland wild flowers as we pushed my younger sister, Susie (born in 1941), in her pram, and I sulkily scuffed my feet.

Many years later I wrote a poem about these walks:

On either side the flinty lane
Name the country flowers again,

In soothing mantra, incantation,
Poppy-wreathed meditation.
Knapweed, scabious, toadflax yellow,
Chicory blue and stinking yarrow,
Nodding harebells, hair-thin stalked,
Where along the Dyke we walked.

Nature was also there to be exploited – wild strawberries grew where we picnicked and I was enchanted by fairy rings in the short turf. When blackberries and rosehips were in season they had to be picked and made into jams and jellies.

One of my favourite walks was down the lane to what we called the 'swinging tree' field where there were ancient beech trees set in lush pasture with long low branches on which we could lie and make them bounce up and down. Inevitably, I also climbed the trees, as I did the drainpipes of my grandmother's house (and once – I shudder now to think of it – walked the length of the long rail of the upstairs balcony that curved round half the house). The 'swinging tree' field was also filled with cowslips and occasionally cows, one of whom licked my ear with her rough tongue when I was intent on creating a chain of cowslips.

We always had pets. I had much-loved Rose, a water spaniel/Kerry Blue cross, black and curly haired, who came to us when I was twelve months old, so I grew up with her. Dinah had a succession of cats, most of which came to an untimely end or ran away to the farm down below. The one ginger tom that survived exhausted himself through being the only unneutered male for miles around. We also had chickens and for a time had a goat called Whitebell in imitation of the school goat called Bluebell. She had a kid which, being male, mysteriously vanished (presumably sold to a butcher) so that we could have her milk. Unfortunately she refused to be milked by my mother and kicked the bucket over, so I think the experiment was rapidly abandoned.

Summer days, memories of which elide into much later summer holidays during my teenage years, were often spent swimming in or rowing on the Thames. During the war we often had to manage the lock gates ourselves and there were very few other boats on the river. One year there were two beautiful black Australian swans on the river but they were soon harried away by the much larger mute swans whom we were told could break an arm with a blow from their wings. My parents, who had spent their honeymoon in a punt on the river, were competent rowers and soon assumed that we would be safe by ourselves, although in later years Dinah tended to daydream when in charge of the tiller ropes, so to my fury I would constantly find myself rowing straight from one bank to the other.

We were little touched by the war. Living in the country, we had our own vegetables and the farm down below supplied milk. Occasionally there would be parcels of dried fruit from distant cousins in Australia. However, we did live near the large wartime aerodrome at Benson and saw large flights of bombers taking off for Germany. On one occasion one crashed when almost home and Dinah and I saw the crew parachuting down over Grimms Dyke, although the pilot was killed when the plane crashed half a mile away, bringing down a large chunk of the kitchen ceiling which narrowly missed my grandmother. With the callousness of children we were unaffected by this tragedy and merely excited when we subsequently saw the wreckage of the plane.

In early 1944 we moved to the much more restrictive surroundings of our own suburban house at 38 Carpenter's Wood Drive in Chorleywood in Hertfordshire. My father was now permanently based in London on MI6 business and commuted daily. Chorleywood was and is on the Metropolitan line, but in those days it was only electrified as far as Rickmansworth, so the train had to wait there for a change of engines as the electric engine was replaced by a panting steam engine. This change of location meant another new school for me and Dinah. We went to a PNEU (Parents' National Education Union) school within walking distance of our home and had to wear a rather boring grey uniform with little hats with brown and blue ribbons. I remember little about the school except that the meals were wartime fare – black potatoes and soggy cabbage – and that one of the strictest teachers had 'a nervous breakdown'; with the ignorance and arrogance of an eight-year-old I thought she was the last person one could describe as 'nervous'.

The one delightful feature of our house in Chorleywood was that at the top of our steep garden there was a large wood filled with bluebells in spring, plus wild cherry trees and sweet chestnuts as well as great beeches, larches and wild raspberries. It became the playground for me and my mainly male friends, especially Stuart and Stella and John, where we became a gang in rivalry with the boys in another street called Main Way, and we wrestled and played cricket in the internal 'Paddock' in the wood where we had to avoid the occasional cowpats.

The other great pleasure of this time was that it was only a short train journey to my paternal grandparents' house in Northwood, where my grandfather Papoose (Oscar Hilton) practised as a GP. Their house, the 'Corner House', contained my grandfather's surgery and waiting room. In the hall with a large red Turkey carpet there was an old-fashioned weighing machine with a platform on which one stood and a balance arm with a moveable weight.

As the favourite and eldest grandchild I was probably very spoilt (on my mother's side of the family I had many older cousins) but I welcomed the strict rules (one must always have bread and butter before one can have a slice of cake) in contrast to my own family's rather laissez-faire attitudes. Granny also had strict ideas about regular daily bowel movements, something about which my parents never enquired, which she called 'Good Grunties' – an expression which I still remember with embarrassment.

Granny insisted that I learn to both knit and crochet and do cross-stitch (a discipline that she had imposed on all three of her sons, who had each crocheted an egg cosy). I struggled with large wooden knitting needles and have never mastered the art of knitting. She also taught me to play croquet (two of her sisters had been croquet champions) – a family passion and a skill with which I have sometimes surprised people later in life. Granny always had a great enthusiasm for nature; when she was in her eighties she still delighted in primroses and bluebells in the lanes of Dorset where I drove her rather slowly in my grandfather's old Vauxhall car. On a walk in Northwood she showed me coltsfoots growing on the railway embankment – a memory evoked (like Proust's madeleine biscuit) on a March day seventy years later at the Barnes Wetland Centre when I saw coltsfoots growing on a bank beside the path.

There were large gardens to the front and back of the house and a pond containing newts – the beginning of a lifelong love affair with amphibians. My grandfather (normally a rather aloof and impatient man) showed me disturbing slides of insects under his microscope and (he was a fellow of the Zoological Society) took me to London Zoo, where I went for a walk with a king penguin in the famous art deco pool. I was also allowed to stroke what I think was a tiger cub behind the public cages. On another occasion he took me to the Natural History Museum when the central hall still contained the cast of a diplodocus skeleton with its long misplaced tail and a family of stuffed elephants in front of the central staircase. The model of the blue whale was, then as now, truly astonishing.

At the 'Corner House' there were other delights – the books and journals of an earlier generation – the Boys Own Paper, an edition of Baden Powell's 'Scouting for Boys', tales of patriotic adventure by Henty and Ballantine and Rider Haggard. This was in contrast to the books at 'Crowsnest' – fairy stories, often illustrated by Arthur Rackham, by Grimm, Andersen and, much loved, George Macdonald's two books about the Princess and Curdie – and weighty classics such as *Robinson Crusoe* and works by Dickens. On all the family bookshelves on both sides of the family there were Lewis Carroll and Edward Lear – read to us at an early age and then constantly reread so that I have much of the poetry by heart, and I also absorbed a Victorian model of ethical behaviour and a desire for adventure.

Also at the Corner House there was a drawer in the tallboy in the dining room containing the 'museum' – the preserved outer shells of armadillos, tiny dry infant crocodiles, fossils and a piece of withered bread said to have survived the 1870 siege of Paris! I also remember the deep humiliation at the age of about four or five when I didn't understand the forfeit in some game when I was told I had to bite 'an inch off the poker'(i.e. bite an inch away from the poker) and all the grown-ups laughed at me and I burst into tears. I never did like to admit to ignorance and when asked a difficult question would retreat, as described earlier, into saying my doll, Baby Batty, 'has a book about it'.

The result of my extensive diet of reading rather old-fashioned books was that I longed for travel and adventure. I imagined myself shipwrecked on an island like Robinson Crusoe, Jim Hawkins or the family on Coral Island eating breadfruit and making clothes out of palm fronds. At an early age I declared that I wanted to be 'an explorer' (during a brief moment of religious belief I thought the answer was to become a missionary!). I was called 'a tomboy' and loved wearing shorts – much to the displeasure of my grandmother, who said they were not suitable for the female figure. I also had a weekly order at the local newsagent/sweet shop for a magazine called *The Wizard* which included tales of adventure, and in particular a character called 'Wilson' who was a sort of hyper-athlete like Superman. On one occasion when I went to collect the magazine the woman in the shop said it was not for girls – a remark that I deeply resented and which perhaps accounts for my only episode of shoplifting – I stole a packet of Wrigley's chewing gum from the shop.

3

GREECE

In 1945, as the war ended (I remember still being frightened that Hitler might not be dead after all!), my father spent a few months in Istanbul and was then posted to Athens. We were to follow him out at the end of the year, which was a fraught one for my mother as she had measles and all three of us caught it. All the while, she tried to cope with packing up the house, which was to be let to an American army sergeant. I was warned that measles might make you go blind and that I was not to read – a serious deprivation – and I was caught reading with a torch under my bedclothes.

Uncle Roger, who had been captured after the abortive raid on Dieppe and had spent much of the war as a prisoner, eventually forced on desperate marches to escape the Russian army, came to help pack the books which were put in the loft for safe keeping. He was very thin and no doubt traumatised by his experiences but was largely withdrawn and silent – not as I remember him later, when he became a well-known abstract artist, drank too much and was bitterly sarcastic about my chosen profession.

It probably did not help that he had been arrested more than once and disqualified for drink-driving.

As always, whilst my mother was packing for Greece, I was expected to be very grown-up and responsible. I was sent up to London alone at the age of nine to catch a bus from Baker Street to St John's Wood for an appointment with our rather terrifying dentist, who had no patience with tears of pain. I tried to distract myself by looking at the pair of corkscrewed bay trees that he had in his garden. There were also times when I was left for a few hours in charge of my two young sisters and I found that frightening as there had been an occasion (when my mother was present) when Dinah had stood too close to the gas fire and set her nightdress alight. My mother quickly beat out the flames but I was transfixed by shock and kept thinking she should be rolled up in a carpet.

On the December night in 1945 before we flew off from Blackbushe airport in Hampshire, we spent a night in the army barracks there. We took off in a Dakota at dawn with a red sun rising. I knew that three Dakotas, worn out by wartime service, had crashed that year and was both frightened and very excited. The plane had inward-facing metal seats on either side of the aisle and there was a heap of mailbags in one corner on which I spent some of the flight. We stopped for refuelling in Paris where I tried to speak French to an unfriendly waitress to ask for a bun and a cup of tea but ended up having to point to what I wanted. My mother, who spoke fluent French, was occupied with my two small sisters. We then carried on to Naples, flying very low over the Alps so that I could see down into the winding valleys and fields. It was bitterly cold in the plane, so the only time in my life I have had chilblains was in Naples!

Because we had a low level of priority (military rule still applied), we then spent two nights in a bare hotel in Naples. I was very jealous of those who came in on the plane after us who had been flown round the top of Vesuvius before landing. Vesuvius was still smoking after the previous year's eruption – all I knew about Naples was the expression 'See Naples and Die', which was very confusing for a nine-year-old! In the hotel, a great empty barrack, all three of us children had to share a bed, head to toe, as there was only one blanket between us. The cold streets of Naples the following day were full of ruined buildings and rubble-strewn spaces. I saw a man urinating on a bombsite and, particularly shocking, a boy with a crutch and the naked footless stump of his leg protruding from his ragged trousers. The churches were full of people huddled together for warmth.

From Naples we flew on to Bari in another Dakota, but this one had canvas seats like deckchairs. The hotel in Bari, in complete contrast to the one in Naples, was centrally heated, art deco in style, and full of American soldiers. We were befriended by an English man we called 'the fur-coat man' because he wore a flying jacket with a fur collar; he was also flying on to Greece, where we saw him from time to time, although I never did learn his real name. In Bari he arranged for us to go and see a hypnotist's show in a theatre packed with British and American troops, some of whom were induced to go on stage to do silly things like riding imaginary bicycles. My sister Dinah, aged seven, thought she had been hypnotised when the audience were told to clasp their hands above their heads and that they wouldn't be able to unclasp them until given a word of command. I was more sceptical.

We eventually arrived in a cold, bleak Athens in mid-December 1945 after a week of travelling. It snowed shortly after our arrival – a rare occurrence in that climate. I have no recollection of a Christmas celebration. For the first three months that we were in Greece we lived in the Grande Bretagne Hotel along with many other diplomatic families – Susie, aged four, deeply offended the Russian Ambassador by pulling his beard too hard when picked up and encouraged to kiss him – a serious diplomatic incident! After the Germans had left the previous year there had been bitter fighting in the streets of Athens between the communist partisans and those who wanted a return to the pre-war monarchy. Dinah and I were reprimanded by our father for tapping out the rhythm of the royalist slogan on the door of our room – a dangerous excursion into politics when we were supposed to be neutral! The royalist crowds outside the hotel in the square opposite the Royal Palace (now the seat of the Greek parliament) had been chanting the slogan all day – '*é, é, érchetai*' (he's coming, he's coming) – and it was infectious. The monarchy did indeed come back, and some months later we had tea with the young princesses.

Whilst living in the Grande Bretagne both my sisters had serious stomach upsets and my distracted mother sent me out alone into the streets of Athens to buy oranges – it was always assumed that I would somehow cope without a word of Greek. Food in the hotel was very limited – I vividly remember the loathsome creamed spinach with a poached egg on top. On one occasion in the hotel we three children were exploring and found the kitchens and the American Bar where they were serving luxuries like lobster. We were rapidly chased back to our rooms. On one occasion Dinah and I drank from a bottle in our bedroom thinking it was water and were surprised to find it was ouzo! Many Greeks at this time were starving, and later, when we moved out to our own house in a village called Nea Kifissia (now a suburb of Athens), we received a weekly box of army rations – mostly cornflakes, corned beef, and tins of Carnation milk. Moussaka made with corned beef is delicious!

Once the weather improved we began to go for walks about Athens: up the steep climb of Mount Lycabettus, a zigzag path through the prickly pears; up onto the Acropolis, where with no other tourists we could wander at will through the Parthenon and the Erechtheion and sit looking down on Athens spread before us, and directly below the delightfully named 'Tower of the Four Winds', a water clock. One beautiful evening with a full moon we went to a concert in the almost complete Roman amphitheatre. A daily delight was the changing of the guard in front of the Royal Palace with the Evzones' swirling white kilts and the black pompoms on their curved shoes. After watching the ceremony we would walk into the Palace Gardens full of palms and other exotic trees and a caged and bad-tempered sulphur-crested cockatoo which shrieked and had a reputation for biting unwary fingers. Once, horrifyingly, we came across a group of Greek boys getting a toad to smoke a cigarette.

My mother did her best to provide us with something to occupy our time. We went to dancing lessons – ballet and 'music and movement' – and went for walks with Mademoiselle France, who was supposed to teach us to speak French. Many upper-class Greeks in those days spoke French as their first language, and it was the diplomatic language throughout the Middle East. I don't think I learnt very much from her except that my French accent is, I am told, Middle Eastern rather than British. One of the few gastronomic delights was yogurt, which we bought direct from the dairy in little brown earthenware bowls (these had to be returned). They had a thick skin of delicious cream on the surface which we sprinkled with sugar. I was also introduced to pistachios and other nuts sold freshly roasted by a man on a bicycle with a portable stove. I have been passionate about nuts ever since.

At Easter we were driven up to Delphi to stay for a week. Apart from my father there were other men from the British Embassy. The journey was chiefly remarkable for the state of the road – swept away in places by war or avalanches so that we had to cross missing sections on precarious planks with a mountain on one side and a sheer drop on the other. Basil Boothby (later to become an ambassador) wanted to take over the driving and got into a furious argument with the driver, who produced a threatening knife. Basil was persuaded to desist. We had lunch at a wayside inn where I was surprised to have yogurt served with meat. In Delphi there was only one other tourist in our bare hotel, an Englishwoman who offered me some of her pomegranate, a new experience which I did not much enjoy. Food consisted chiefly of eggs and the inevitable cornflakes and tinned milk we had brought with us. One precious chicken was sacrificed for us during the week.

Delphi was magical. My ten-year-old imagination could feed on classical ruins, oracles, drugged priestesses, and prophesies. The rocky landscape soaring above the ruins and the plunge below with a distant glimpse of the blue Gulf of Corinth were truly beautiful. It was my first real encounter with mountains, and then on an early walk there was a golden eagle, as tall as myself, sitting majestically by the side of the road! One day we hired donkeys and trekked steeply down below the shelf of rock on which Delphi is perched. On the slope below there were waterfalls, a sacred 'bottomless' pool, and olive trees and a carpet of anemones – pink and white with an occasional brilliant scarlet flower.

On our return to Athens in spring 1946 we moved out to our modest but modern bungalow in the countryside. The road to it consisted largely of hard-baked mud ruts but the area had ambitions to be a smart suburb and there were little mulberry trees planted alongside some of the neighbouring streets. Because the Germans had left their cars behind when they hurriedly departed, the Embassy staff could take their pick and we had an open-topped Mercedes sports car – although a four-wheel-drive car would have been more practical. We regularly went to the seaside, where I learnt to swim and watched Greek boys catching and cooking crabs. We made an expedition to the scene of the Battle of Marathon, chiefly remembered by me for my first sight of wild cyclamen growing out of the bare turf.

Around our house there were no wildflowers but there were many tortoises to be carried back to our small bare garden, and lizards, mostly little brown ones with an occasional large brilliant green one. The tortoises usually had ticks attached to their armpits, which I tried to deal with by putting salt on them – this was temporarily effective until they wandered back out into the surrounding countryside. Our maid (we usually had a servant in Greece) did not like the tortoises and kicked off one that I had placed on the kitchen steps, in consequence of which I learned several Greek swear words. The fauna that I did not like were the four-inch poisonous centipedes, striped yellow and black like tigers with twin rows of claws. One day I saw a woman whose arm had been poisoned by a centipede and it was swollen to twice its natural size. The centipedes could be found under stones in the garden, and on one awful occasion when I was in bed with a cold my mother shook out a napkin and a centipede fell out – they had been nesting in the airing cupboard. I have rarely moved so fast in my life and have had a horror of centipedes, even small garden ones, ever since.

Next to our house lived a Greek family, the Lithakis, who had two young teenage sons, Nico and Yannis, with whom we played and regularly swam in their large tank, which was theoretically used for irrigating their small garden, although I cannot remember much growing there. Our garden only had thin grass and some scrubby pine trees. Dinah with her blonde hair was a particular favourite of theirs. They also had a dog, Bobby, who kept having large litters of puppies. We had two: Pluto, a delightful blond puppy who soon succumbed to distemper (Dinah accused me of hard-heartedness because I was not weeping over his death); and Chocolat, who was much tougher and soon ran away and was seen scavenging in the centre of the small town.

The area was open countryside with a small rocky stream about a mile away where we bathed naked and where there were little black water tortoises under the stones. We got into trouble for eating a farmer's figs and one glorious day we came across a neglected apricot tree whose fruit lay scattered on the ground beneath. My lasting passion for apricots recently led me to plant an apricot on my allotment, but alas its few fruits are usually stolen by squirrels. Our drinking water was kept in porous earthenware jars on the veranda so that evaporation would keep it cool. Every so often it was my task to take the jar to a nearby farm with a terrifying but chained dog, to draw fresh water out of the well. In the summer we slept out in the cool of our garden on camp beds under the pine trees and were occasionally woken by men shouting as the intermittent irrigation water came down the nearby channel.

Less idyllic was the fact that the buildings housing the lunatic asylum were only half a mile away and we could sometimes hear the screams of the inmates. I was frightened to walk past but my mother painted several small oil paintings with the buildings looking tranquil in the foreground and Mount Parnitha brooding in the background. Greek children were also casually cruel to animals, killing harmless snakes and tying long thread to cicadas so that they could only fly in small buzzing circles. I was horrified but lacked the courage to protest.

After Delphi we had other expeditions. One summer we went to the island of Poros, which was chiefly memorable for the return journey. We were caught in a sudden storm and the ship's steering gear failed so that we wallowed in the trough of waves as high as the ship. My mother was not a good sailor and was coping with her own nausea. Aged ten, in arrogant, stiff-upper-lip fashion, I was scornful of the other passengers who were sobbing, telling their beads and being sick over the luggage. Eventually another ferry came out and towed us into harbour on another island where we spent the night. We also went to Mycenae by train across the Gulf of Corinth and stayed in a little pension before going up to the citadel on the backs of donkeys. Pau-Pau and Aunt Saintie were with us so it must have been just before my brother, Tom, was born in the spring of 1947. We had the site, the beehive and shaft tombs to ourselves where now there are troupes of tourists and a large coach park. I was impressed by the lion gateway, but, knowing little of the *Iliad* and *Odyssey*, it was only on a visit many years later that my imagination was appropriately stirred.

For the whole of 1946 I had no formal schooling. Mademoiselle France came occasionally to teach us some French, and I always read extensively. My parents had brought a small library of poetry books, which proved useful later when I wrote pastiches for entertainment nights at the Police College or for travelling companions to India and China, and for painting groups in Italy. I did not think about the oddity of not going to school, nor about the lack of companions of my own age throughout my childhood, but it may account for my difficulty in feeling part of any group and not being good at small talk.

At the beginning of 1947, a British Army School was opened in Kifissia in a large house with an overgrown garden. Dinah and I walked there every day. There were only a couple of dozen pupils – the children of British Army officers and diplomats. The teaching was limited – I remember drawing a church with accurate perspective and vanishing points. I was told off for writing doggerel in my notebook and was mocked because I said New York was the capital of America. Very oddly, we were examined naked by an army doctor and prodded in various places. A chief excitement was a family of baby hedgehogs which narrowly escaped a grass fire. My nascent feminism was aroused by one of the male teachers who said that women cannot judge distances and by the fact that the boys were taken into Athens for carpentry lessons denied to the girls. My feelings about condescending male patronage had previously been stirred when staying at Granny's and looking at a picture of a sinking ship with a caption that said, 'Women and children first.' Indignant, I said that I wanted an equal right to go down with the ship!

In the spring of 1947, when Pau-Pau was staying with us, my brother Tom was born in April. When Pau-Pau and I visited my mother in hospital I read a note (not meant for me) which said,

'He has a hare lip'. I did not understand this, but it seemed shocking. Tom's hare lip and cleft palate meant that he had to be fed with a teaspoon and subsequently resulted in many stays in hospital for restorative operations. My father went back to England in June and we followed soon after, flying in luxury this time in a passenger plane, a Skymaster, and refuelling in Geneva. In Amsterdam we changed planes and eventually arrived back in London, landing at Northolt as Heathrow did not yet exist.

4

BEDALES

We came home to England from Greece in June 1947 and stayed
with both sets of grandparents. Whilst we were at Pau-Pau's my
father had a serious discussion with me about my future schooling.
I remember the tense discussion took place in the black wooden
hut that my grandmother used for wood-block printing. My
father said the choices were a mediocre day school or a year at a
secondary modern and then a good boarding school, like Bedales,
for the rest of my teenage years. I had already insisted that I did
not want to go to an all girls' school as I thought that boys had a
more interesting and adventurous time and I rather despised the
idea of being exclusively feminine, which I associated with being
weak and lacking in initiative (I had absorbed all the stereotypes
of the Boys' Own papers). I was also keen to be a boarder as
there were always tensions at home as my mother was not
suited to domestic life (she had grown up with servants) and was
preoccupied with my brother Tom's problems.

I am not sure why my father thought it appropriate to give the
choice to an eleven-year-old with no school friends or knowledge

of the school system. I nervously chose the second option. As I had to wait until the following Easter for extensive interviews at Bedales, I went to the local secondary modern school in Chesham in September. Before my weekend of tests my mother admonished me not to say 'I don't mind' when offered a choice. Had I been too biddable? I don't remember any other advice.

My year at the secondary modern school, alas, reinforced the effect of a year without school in Greece as I was able, with little effort, to be near the top of the class. I did not fit in – I had no knowledge of film stars or of the games the other girls played, and it was my first experience of differences in social class. They showed no interest in me so I told ridiculous lies – that I was one of the people who broke the ice in the Serpentine on Christmas Day and that I had read the Bible from cover to cover. I must have been very unhappy. The feeling of being an outsider is a common experience, but I had had little opportunity to belong to a group. This sense of detachment and perhaps lack of empathy was probably useful in the police service later.

Despite the difficulties, I am grateful for having been made to learn some poetry by heart, including Housman's 'Loveliest of Trees', which had particular resonance when the wild cherries in the wood behind our house came into flower (and which I quoted recently when monitoring elections in Tbilisi when all the cherries lining the streets were in flower – my fellow monitor said, 'The Japanese would agree!'). Otherwise, living in a suburban setting with three younger siblings at home and my mother very preoccupied with my infant brother was a sad contrast to the glory that was Greece. The few friends that I had had before we went to Greece were growing up. Stuart Nichols was taking his scouting very seriously (he later became a headmaster), while John was humorous when he hung by his heels from the luggage rack on the train that we took to Chesham each day but had few other amusing traits. Wendy and Stella were already beginning to think about boyfriends, and I had no interest in clothes or makeup. They tolerated me but we were not close and drifted apart once I was away at Bedales for most of the year.

At Easter 1948 I had a two-day extended interview at Bedales, with several members of staff, including the art mistress, Betty Tweed, who seemed to like what I painted, and Paul Bloomfield, a friend of my father's. I also had a wrestling match with Bridget Brown, who later became one of my closest friends. I was accepted into Bedales. Several people who worked with my father in the Foreign Office also had children at the school. There was gentle, willowy Mary O'Brien, several years older than me, who later became a Senior Wrangler in Mathematics at Oxford University (I used her as an example when I was later a governor at Bedales and had a furious argument with the maths teacher who said women were genetically unable to do maths; why was he at a co-ed school?).

Another friend was Carol Asphodel (after her godmother) Cohen, who spoke beautiful French and was always late for lessons because she was reading something esoteric but could excuse herself with great courtesy. She was hopeless at games and sometimes as a plump teenager I was paired with her for tennis – my game did not improve as she rarely got the ball back over the net. I greatly disliked being seen as physically feeble as it did not fit with my self-image as an intrepid explorer! I did have some physical skills; I could climb ropes in the gym and I loved playing cricket as I did later for the Metropolitan Police Women's Cricket Team.

Bedales had been founded by J. H. Baddeley in 1893 as a reaction against the limited curriculum of the boys' public schools. Within six years, girls (initially the sisters of boys already there) were also admitted and the same regime applied to both sexes. Because the school was non-denominational and not tied to any religion, there were a number of Jewish children and for two years a lovely Buddhist boy from Indonesia. Baddeley thought that girls, like boys, should be beaten, although this form of punishment was soon abandoned in favour of 'extra work', usually some form of manual labour (I was once set to cleaning all the keys of a piano as a punishment for missing a music lesson). From the start there was an emphasis on language, literature, art and music, and many of the school buildings and furniture were in the Arts and Craft tradition – the library and assembly hall being modelled on tithe barns with great oak beams. The school also had a 150-acre farm and we were expected to help with harvesting and caring for the cows and pigs – 'outdoor work' continued to occupy an afternoon a week, and I remember sawing logs and harvesting cabbages and potatoes on a freezing day. On the whole I preferred this to team games such as lacrosse and netball. Between the world wars, Bedalians had also constructed the wooden cricket pavilion like a miniature tithe barn. The 'spirit that built the pav' was an oft-touted aphorism, along with the school motto 'Work of each for weal of all' to encourage us to be tougher and more innovative.

The school ethos was that all people, regardless of race or religion, were to be valued as much for their practical or artistic skills as they would be for showing intellectual prowess. As a relic of the early Spartan spirit of the school, we had cold baths every morning. These were more like a cold dip. I would hand my towel to a waiting prefect, leap in and out of a bath full of cold water, take my towel back from the prefect and run shivering back to my dormitory. The boys in addition had a morning run before breakfast – one occasion when I had no envy of the other sex. In the afternoons, after games, we did have communal hot showers – it was often the only way to get warm.

The school had a very high staff-to-student ratio and there were many unusual and long-established members of staff with powerful personalities. We were encouraged to call them by their first names and shake the hands of those members of staff present at the end of each evening's assembly. There was the maths teacher, Anthony Gillingham, who was a communist and sang beautifully in the annual Gilbert and Sullivan performances in the local town, Petersfield. He and his wife had five children (and allegedly she had also had several miscarriages). He later deserted her for another, younger woman. Rachel Carey Field, a short, plump woman, was the rather terrifying speech mistress. She once made me stand on the stage and recite a joke – I knew no jokes and was struck dumb. She directed the termly school plays and usually became hysterical with rage two or three days before each performance, which had the actors quivering and abashed but motivated some memorable acting. I later became assistant 'props' to Andrea Millington (we created a wonderful papier-maché fish for the banquet in *Le Bourgeois gentilhomme*) and Rachel treated me with affection. Sadly she later developed diabetes, went blind and died comparatively young.

Other members of staff were more conventional. The headmaster, Hector Jacks, was a Unitarian. His predecessor, Freddie Meier, had been greatly loved but had let academic standards in the school decline, so Hector's more rigorous regime was initially unpopular.

He was gently mocked for his inability to say his 'Rs'. Each autumn, when the apple trees in the orchard were heavy with fruit, he would address the whole school, saying, 'Hands off the fwoot.' Joyce Caiger Smith, the girls' housemistress, was stuffily conventional and gave a prayer book to those few girls who were confirmed in the Church of England. I was already a confirmed atheist by this time.

In my first dormitory that autumn of 1948 we had as our dorm boss Anthea Hume, whom I adored for the next two years. She was sixteen and was later to win major scholarships to both Oxford and Cambridge. She in turn was passionate about the English teacher, Mary Morris, who had beautiful, long, flowing red hair. I think I fell in love with Anthea when she sang in a musical that the senior girls put on for the retiring girls' matron, Miss Rogers (chiefly remarkable for her small yappy dog). Anthea played the part of a giant and sang 'Early One Morning', which had the chorus:

> I chopped her and roasted her,
> With butter toasted her
> No more did that maiden sing in the valley below

My earlier erotic feelings had had no settled object; a girl seen from a distance with great vividness, another who had lent me her tan leather jacket when I was cold on a car journey in Greece. Anthea was kind to me, sympathetic when on one occasion I was in the sick bay and burst into tears. When, greatly daring, I wrote a letter to her during one summer holiday, she replied quoting Horatio's advice to Hamlet about not being passion's slave! I do not remember what I had written that provoked that reply.

I met her many years later when she was depressed and seeing a therapist and without the vitality she displayed as a teenager when she had stood in a mock election for the Labour Party. She later did a PhD on Tyndall and became a university lecturer and distinguished academic.

The sexual atmosphere at Bedales was completely heterosexual, although there was one day boy, David Sykes, in my year whose campy gay mannerisms were never commented upon – perhaps because of his apparent self-confidence and perpetual cheerfulness. He was also a very good artist. The standard gossip was all about which boy was 'going with' which girl, and there were dark rumours about what went on in the grove of chestnut trees above the playing fields. When I expressed my disapproval of this, my friend Mary called me a 'prig', which was hurtful. I was very naïve about sex and thought that homosexuals were exclusively male, as several of my fathers' friends – Anthony Blunt and my godfather, Moore Crosthwaite, were homosexual. I did not understand the sniggering about the games mistress, Mary Bulpit, who was living with a woman. Later, when I was sixteen or seventeen, I did come to define myself as homosexual through reading books such as Radclyffe Hall's *The Well of Loneliness*, Colette's Claudine novels and Virginia Woolf's *Orlando* – once described as the longest love letter ever written. It is hard to imagine given the febrile interest in sexuality today, but no one expressed an interest in my love life. We mostly wore school uniform – a nice red blazer and a shapeless green pinafore dress – so my lack of interest in clothes was not too apparent.

Overt expressions of physical desire between the boys and girls went little beyond holding hands and no one became pregnant during my six years at Bedales. The girls' house, Steephurst, was in a completely separate building from the main school. The thrice-termly school dances were a misery for me, and I think for all the less extroverted of both genders. Waiting on one side of the dance floor for one of the self-conscious boys to cross over and to ask formally for a dance was a painful ordeal. More modern dance styles where everyone can join in are much easier to cope with and I have even found them enjoyable! In the end I opted out completely and hid in the library where I tried to cheer myself up by reading the works of P. G. Wodehouse and Dornford Yates.

My reluctance to apply myself to formal classwork continued (I have invented several explanations since: fear of failure, not being clever enough to please my father, deliberately opting out of competition). School report after school report said that I did not try hard enough, but I did not really know how to apply myself to a serious course of study (when, much later, I took the foreigners' language course at the Sorbonne I found for the first time that I did enjoy the rigours of formal learning). I passed six O Levels without doing any work but kept failing Latin – an essential prerequisite for the older universities – and thought I could also pass my three A Levels without doing any work – only to be sadly disillusioned. Latin was taught by Cyril King, a gentle man who had suffered shell-shock in the First World War. My contemporaries had none of my problems, and my friends Bridget Brown, Mary Selwyn-Clarke and Carol Cohen all went on to Oxford. I longed to go too as both my parents had been there.

The other subject that I failed at O Level was general science, which was a surprise because I loved and was good at the biology and physics elements (I have since become a regular member of the House of Lords Science and Technology Committee).

However, the third element was chemistry and one had to pass in all three parts. The chemistry teacher was a dour Scot called Martin Prain who had no time for girls. The boys were encouraged to go to his evening activities where they grew lovely crystals and did explosive experiments. It would have been better if I had done biology or physics as single subjects.

Bedales provided me with a wide-ranging education. I read a great deal, but little of it was connected with the formal curriculum. As a school librarian I was allotted a bay upstairs in the barn-like library with its magnificent oak beams. My bay, under the Dewey system of classification, was the psychology and philosophy bay, so I read Freud, Bertrand Russell's *History of Western Philosophy*, Sartre's *Existentialism*, Frazer's *The Golden Bough* and other books that I had heard referred to, such as C. S. Lewis's *The Allegory of Love* and G. M. Heard's *Experiment with Time* (which was fun and echoed recently by Kate Atkinson's novel *Life after Life* where the protagonist has several parallel lives) and his *Third Morality* (which I did not understand). The school had the great good fortune to be addressed by Fred Hoyle and Geoffrey Hoyland, so I knew at an early stage the rival claims of the Steady State versus Big Bang theories of cosmology and I took to reading books about astronomy and enjoyed the terminology of 'red dwarfs' and 'white giants'. Tangentially connected to my history A Level I also read the whole of Runciman's *History of the Crusades*.

Outside of formal lessons there were evening activities (such as Martin Prain's chemistry demonstrations). Bedales, alas, still ascribed gender roles for some formal lessons, and whilst girls had to do cookery and sewing, boys did carpentry with 'Biff Barker'. I resented this distinction and used to deliberately lose my sewing and spend the lesson allegedly looking for it – one hot summer's day lying on my back concealed in the blackcurrant bushes. However, evening activities were unisex so I made a bookcase (which I still have) and several little copper bowls. I failed to master the use of a lathe, however, and after having produced an uneven spiral rather than a smooth column of wood that was supposed to become egg cups, I abandoned carpentry. I could hold my own in painting and drawing lessons, and passed at O Level; these lessons were always a solace and I felt comfortable in the art room. I also contributed some articles to the school magazine and won second prize in the Macdonald Essay Competition with an essay on the evils of tolerance. I was clearly a revolutionary at heart!

Music played a very important part in the life of the school and most of its pupils. For six months I made a desultory effort to play the clarinet but soon gave up. I was mocked for not being able to sing in tune and sitting among the altos I often found it easier to sing the main tune with the tenors behind me rather than attempt a counterpoint. I felt very unhappy at lunch one day when two other people began singing little snatches of tune to each other. My friend Bridget tried to teach me to sing 'God Save the Queen' in tune but soon gave up. On another occasion I was hurt and jealous when she went on a special trip to hear monks singing plainsong and told me I would not appreciate it.

I was not impervious to the sound of the human voice or the pleasures of singing. I have since become an enthusiastic opera fan. On Saturday mornings we had 'Whole School Singing', which I loved, and we sang choruses from Haydn's *Creation* and other oratorios, sea shanties, and Gilbert and Sullivan. Early in my school life we had a fleeting visit by Paul Robeson when he was on a tour of Britain. I had no knowledge of his greatness but the warmth of his voice was unforgettable and he soon had the whole school enthusiastically singing 'My little baby loves shortening bread'. On another occasion a small group of us sat on the floor of the Crumps' living room in her house in the village to see C. Day Lewis play the piano and sing a song that began 'My heart was as light as the seed of a thistle...' Barbara Crump was the school librarian and her husband Geoffrey was a theatre producer in London. We had two wonderful outings in successive years to hear the St Matthew Passion sung at the Albert Hall and were taken up to London to see Shakespeare plays at the Old Vic.

On Sunday afternoons we were expected to go for walks, so I usually went with my regular companions, Bridget Brown and Mary Selwyn-Clarke. Mary's father, Sir Selwyn Selwyn-Clarke, was a distinguished doctor and colonial governor in the Seychelles who had been interred by the Japanese during the war and had acted with great bravery tending his fellow prisoners. Mary and her mother had also been interred in another camp and Mary's first sight of snow was during our first winter at Bedales.

I went to stay at their grand house in Hampstead several times. Sir Selwyn, a dauntingly severe and upright figure in his dressing gown, brought me morning tea in bed, and did not think much of my manners because I rubbed my face with my hands at breakfast. Mary's mother – such an ill-assorted pair – was a fiercely left-wing activist and LCC councillor. To my embarrassment she refused to stand up for the national anthem at the end of films. Some years later, in 1955, when I was nineteen, I went to Mary's birthday party. I was clad improbably in a long, shiny mauve dress and had a difficult conversation with Sir Selwyn, who expressed astonishment about the vagueness of my future plans.

Impertinently, I said, 'It is better to be sure one is making the right choice!' He had decided from her birth that Mary would become a doctor like he had, and indeed she did.

On our Sunday walks we explored the surrounding countryside, including Strawberry Hanger, Edward Thomas's memorial, the Shoulder of Mutton Hill and Lord Horder's lovely garden where we were allowed to roam at will. On one summer Sunday each year we were expected to stay out for the whole day and at Mary's instigation we set out along the South Downs for a fifteen-mile walk. Bridget and Mary were fast walkers, and Jo Wilson and I were soon trailing far behind – every time they rested we caught up but they would immediately set off again – eventually, after about fifteen miles, in despair, Jo and I came down a hill to a village and caught a bus back to school.

It is difficult to fault the education offered by Bedales since half my year (or 'Block' as we called them) of forty students went on to university – most to Oxford or Cambridge – but I clearly needed a more rigorous regime to overcome the informality or absence of my early schooling. The consequent shame and humiliation that I felt at my failure has turned me into a compulsive autodidact, accumulating (with the help of a police scholarship) two psychology degrees, two diplomas (in criminology and history of art) and, just to prove I could do it, an A Level in French, acquired after twelve months of evening classes.

However, the remarkable consequence of this apparent disaster was that I have had a fascinating career with rare opportunities to experience our society at all levels. The police service not only deals with tragedy and violence but also with great public occasions and celebrations and all aspects of humanity, whether evil, cowardly or heroic. It also, of course, launched me into the

House of Lords when I retired and was appointed by Neil Kinnock to improve the Labour Party's relationship with and attitude to the police service. Traditionally, left-wing parties have had a reflexive anti-police bias so my appointment as a Labour Peer may have come as a surprise to both sides! As I had been a senior police officer for eight years I knew most of the chief constables in the country and so could help to build bridges between the Labour Party and the police service.

I had taken A Levels in maths (probably in emulation of my father's first degree), history (because we were taught by the charismatic Roy Wake) and French (probably for my mother's sake). When the awful results arrived, I remember sitting hunched on the kitchen floor whilst my mother was cooking. She did not understand how devastated I felt as she had cheerfully abandoned Oxford after two terms and had had no ambition to be an academic. I do not remember my father's reaction but I imagine he was very disappointed as he always had great admiration for academic brilliance. I did know that I had not done enough work for the exams, but my apparent inability to pass the Latin O Level meant that I would not be able to go to Oxford or Cambridge. Maybe that depressed me. My rather unworldly family did not think of having me extensively coached.

I went back to Bedales for the final autumn term when everyone else seemed to be applying for universities. I searched a career book for alternatives to being a secretary or a nurse (there were fewer opportunities for women then) and found that the police service required no formal entry qualifications. I clung to this idea as an escape from my fears of a hopeless future. I was sent off for careers advice to be 'nipped' by the NIIP (the National Institute of Industrial Psychology), whose representatives subjected me to various intelligence tests and concluded correctly that I was clever but idle and suggested a career in the WRNS as an alternative to the police service. I don't know whether this suggestion was, like my great-aunt's reaction, class consciousness or not, but I would not have had the same rich range of experiences if I had become a WRN.

Some parts of my sixth-form years at Bedales were very enjoyable. I had earlier indulged in minor delinquencies such as skipping lacrosse practice on cold wet afternoons and joining in midnight feasts in dormitories where we shared crisps and a bottle of cider or possibly some of the illicit hooch produced by a group of rather delinquent boys. I also remember going for a midnight swim and one cloudless summer night on the school playing fields seeing a shower of shooting stars. In my last year, however, I became a prefect, and although I was envious of Bridget, who had become head girl, I enjoyed the prefects' separate common room. There, in companionable friendship, we could make toast and watch tennis matches from our first-floor window with a distant view beyond of the hills of the South Downs, Wardown and Butser (after which the school sports teams were named).

As well as being a prefect I was also a dorm boss, and although we had four or five different girls to share with each term I rather regularly found myself in the same dorm as Priscilla Gourlay, who had terrifying screaming nightmares and regularly sleepwalked. By day she was perfectly sensible. One year I went with her to stay with her mother, the formidable Dr Janet Vaughan, Principal of Somerville College in Oxford. The plan was that on May morning we would take a punt downstream to listen to the choristers on Magdalen Tower welcoming Mayday. Unfortunately neither of us were expert punters, and we ended up a long way from Magdalen revolving in circles and feeling humiliated.

After Anthea Hume, I did not feel passionate about any of the other girls. I was not aware of any other lesbian girls or women, and it was to be many years before I had a love affair.

Despite my failures at Bedales, I had very much enjoyed my time there – I used to count the days of the school holidays before going back to school. Later I spent eight very rewarding years as a one of the school governors.

5

PARIS

If I and my parents had been sensible I should have gone to a crammer to retake my A Levels, but I felt that I had already squandered a great deal of my parents' money and they had my three younger siblings to educate. My father frequently called us his 'pelican daughters', sucking his lifeblood from his breast. I was also depressed and jealous of my friends, who were proceeding triumphantly to university. I therefore had to fill in the time before I could join the police service at the age of twenty. In January 1955 I set off to France to be an au pair but there was a gap of several weeks, so I went to stay with the Douadys, Daniel and Guilhen (my mother's great friend from her artist student days in Paris in the 1930s), and some of their five children. They became a second family to me.

For the first few days my chief friend at Bedales, Bridget, who had been accepted by Oxford to study history, was with me. We had a trip to Versailles, that monstrous palace and its acres of gardens created by the sun king, Louis XIV, before she went on to Switzerland to work in the Pestalozzi village. She subsequently became a probation officer and married a botanist. I was later to be a rather neglectful godmother to her son, Tom. I had explained to her that I had become an atheist at the age of twelve, when I could no longer believe any items in the creed when I was taken to church by my grandmothers, so I could not be responsible for his religious education.

I had visited France and Paris several times before and so knew the Douadys. In about 1948 we had all holidayed together in a small village in the south-west of Brittany on the Gulf of Morbihan (whose many little islands are said to be the flowers dropped from the hair of fairies as they were chased out of France by the giants). The families had not met since before the war. The Douadys were staying in a comfortable farmhouse where we had good lunches including razor-shell fish which we caught by dropping salt into their holes on the beach so that they thought the tide had come in and popped up. However, Guilhen had rented for us nightmare accommodation in a house in the small town with a slaughterhouse in the backyard where squealing pigs and bleating sheep were dispatched at night and blood ran in the yard. We did not get on well with Guilhen's five children. Adrien and Laurence were a bit older than me, and the other three, Clement-Noel, Jerome and Veronique, were younger. I remember for some reason pinning Adrien, who was very small for his age, to the sand and insisting he apologise for something. We also became ill – my mother thought it was the rich diet (including lobster) after wartime restrictions, but I think it was more likely to have been the drinking water that came from the village well. Two of the boys, Adrien and Clement-Noel, later came to stay with us in England, and oddly huddled half-naked in their bathing trunks round the gas fire complaining of the cold, and spat at Nelson's Column when we went to Trafalgar Square. When I was about fifteen I had spent a rather lonely week in Paris helping Laurence, the eldest daughter, with her English homework (a synopsis of *She Stoops to Conquer*) and trying to read *War and Peace*.

During the summer that I was eighteen, during the school holidays I was sent by my parents to Paris with my father's aunt, Gertrude, who was in her eighties, to act as a sort of courier. Auntie Gertie had in her youth been an artist and made enamelled jewellery and had nostalgic memories of her time in France, sketching holidays there with Gordon Craig. She was fat and clothed in tweeds and always wore a shapeless felt hat to disguise having gone bald on top. She was what my father called a 'tuft-hunter' and had an embarrassing fund of resentful stories about famous people, such as mistaking George Bernard Shaw for Yeats (or vice versa) and being surprised that he was offended. She had never forgiven Roger Fry for being more concerned about a Chinese bowl that had fallen and shattered on her head than about her head. When I was with her she also had an embarrassing habit, like the Ancient Mariner, of subjecting busy waitresses to long anecdotes about her previous life in Paris. We had lunch with an old friend of hers, Madame Lloyd, and she did not notice the concerned kerfuffle when I was stung by a wasp. She was too busy talking.

Shamefully, when we were in lovely Chartres Cathedral I abandoned her on the ground floor and fled up one of the towers. At the end of the week I was invited by the Douadys to stay on for Laurence's wedding and Auntie Gertie went on to Boulogne. I danced with Adrien, who was wholly inarticulate at that stage in his life, aged nineteen, but later became an extremely distinguished mathematician and a lively *bon viveur*. When I joined Auntie Gertie in Boulogne some days later I found she had had a difficult time as there was a mayors' convention and the hotels were almost all full, so I felt guilty. I did, however, contribute one small benefit as she said it was the only time she had made a Channel crossing without being sick.

Subsequent holidays with Guilhen were much more enjoyable – staying in their seaside house in Cavalaire-sur-Mer, on the Mediterranean coast near St Tropez; having breakfast under a fig tree and dipping my croissants into a great bowl of milky coffee; looking for pine kernels under the vast Mediterranean pine with Adrien's five-year-old son, Raphael (also to become a distinguished mathematician). The only blight on this holiday was that my mother, unusually, wrote a long letter to me with the latest details of my sister Susie's by then full-blown schizophrenia. In retrospect, I imagine that she was jealous that I was having a good time with Guilhen, whom she saw as her own friend.

In 1963, when I was recovering from a brief and unhappy love affair, I went to Clement-Noel's wedding in Corrèze near Tulle in south-west France. It was December and looked like a scene from a medieval Book of Hours. There was a light hoarfrost on the ground and beneath pale blue skies the oak and chestnut woods were purple and there were pigs snuffling in the litter beneath the trees. The wedding took place in Chaunac, a small village near Tulle, which was Guilhen's ancestral home. There was no room in Guilhen's old farmhouse so I stayed in the curé's room in the small village chateau. The villagers had created a floral bridal arch for Guilhen's house and we had a five-course evening meal with them on the evening before the wedding. Like many French weddings there were two separate ceremonies. One was a church service conducted in Latin in the village church, and the other a civil ceremony in the mayor's office in the town hall in Tulle.

The wedding 'breakfast' was even more magnificent, consisting of seven courses and lasting five hours and ending with the great phallic symbol of a cone of profiteroles. Later in the evening, Guilhen cooked quantities of crepes for everyone over a wood fire.

On another occasion I went to stay with their cousin Annie in a rented house on the west coast of France south of Bordeaux in Les Landes, a place of sand dunes and pine trees where we dug cockles out of the wet sand and ate spider crabs. One day after rain and a full moon we went to look for chanterelles in the pine forest but found none. I have since had more successful hunts for chanterelles in the woods of Pennsylvania and the forests of Sweden where the golden fungi stand out against the leaf litter. I have always loved looking for mushrooms. Seeking the small baby white globes in wet pasture is like a treasure hunt. I have also picked and fried lawyers' wigs, which are delicious, and slices of puffballs.

When I went to Paris in 1955 after leaving school the family were living in a large house conveniently just across the place in front of the railway station of Sceaux – after which the suburban railway south of Paris is called. This provided a convenient twenty-minute ride to the Gare Montparnasse in the heart of the Latin Quarter. I spent several weeks there with the Douadys, probably to Guilhen's dismay, and enjoyed my leisurely breakfasts with her when she corrected my inadequate French with sardonic impatience and asked me about my plans for the future. I think she thought I lacked enterprise and ambition as I was reluctant to explore Paris on my own, and said as a contrast how much they had admired the bravery of English pilots who had flown up the Champs-Élysées during the German occupation of Paris. On one occasion Adrien was, I suspect, coerced into driving me in a tiny *deux-chevaux* Citroen to the forest of Fontainebleau to climb the rocks there. Being slight and agile, he climbed up the rocks with ease whilst I, overweight and out of condition, only managed the easiest of climbs.

When my au pair agent, Judith, took me to see the family who were supposed to be employing me, we found that they had changed their minds. This was a bitter disappointment, as I felt I could no longer trespass on Guilhen's kindness. Judith hurriedly found me a place with an English family where the military father was stationed at SHAPE (Supreme Headquarters Allied Powers in Europe). Fortunately this only lasted three days as the only reading material in the house was copies of *The Lady* and the mother berated her twelve-year-old daughter for reading as it was 'a waste of time'. Judith then found me a French family in the smart sixteenth arrondissement in the west of Paris near the Bois de Boulogne. My duties were to take their five-year-old boy (who had been ill) on walks and to accompany their eight-year-old daughter for two stops on the Metro to and from school each day (I queried this necessity as I had travelled by myself in London at a similar age but was told that it was '*pas convenable*' for her to be unaccompanied). I also had to exercise their large and ugly Airedale, which would drag me uncontrollably down the street. I was briefly attracted to Judith, who was lively, bilingual and half-French and half-English, until I found she was having an affair with her male cousin Yves – much to the disapproval of her grandmother, with whom she lived. Her grandmother's flat was chiefly remarkable for its hydraulic lift, which was very slow and could be speeded up slightly if one pulled on a thick rope that went down through the floor.

I found it difficult to understand the dynamics of the family for whom I worked – there was always tension, and on one occasion the mother beat her daughter for failing to learn her history lesson about the glory that was France. I was in another room and was very distressed but there was nothing I could do. Their surname was 'du Thilleul', which implied an aristocratic background, but Madame unfavourably compared my efforts at ironing with her mother's and every evening I had to prepare the vegetable 'potage' which was allegedly *'bon pour la sante'* and which implied a more modest background. Used as I was to the Douadys' more relaxed attitudes to behaviour (Adrien, for example, always went barefoot on the Metro), I did not feel comfortable there. However, in the evenings they were passionate about playing canasta, which was then very fashionable, and proved useful later when I came to play gin rummy (a very similar card game) at Bow Street on night duty.

At Easter they sent their son to Switzerland for further convalescence and I became redundant, but through Auntie Gertie's old friends I was found lodgings with an elderly French lady, Mlle Long, in her flat in the Rue de Babylone near the Rodin Museum and Les Invalides. Both Mademoiselle Long and Madame Lloyd, whom I had met with Auntie Gertie, had been interned for a time by the Germans. I wonder now whether they were Jewish and if that was the link with Auntie Gertie. The flat was airy and delightful, with a hall decorated with a mural of a fantasy landscape. I had a bedroom and use of the kitchen in return for an English lesson a week for her eight-year-old great-nephew Olivier, whose family lived near the Jardin du Luxembourg. I do not think Olivier, who was delightful, learnt very much English from me but I profited by being able to borrow their books and discovered Colette, who considerably enhanced my sex education.

I was living on £2 a week at this time (money values were very different) – £1 for food and £1 for Metro tickets. I mostly lived on cheese and potatoes, but this was supplemented by free lunches three times a week as a student at the Sorbonne, where I was studying a course in French for foreigners. Lunch in the students' canteen came on a metal tray with dented compartments into which were dumped rather pallid selections of meat, potatoes, veg and pudding. Haute cuisine it was not. On Sundays I gorged myself on lunch with the Douadys. One evening a week I had supper with Stephen Gilbert (whose father designed *Eros* on Piccadilly Circus) and his wife and small daughter. Stephen had trained as an architect so probably knew my father but I think the connection was more likely to have dated from the time when my mother and Uncle Roger had been art students in Paris in the thirties.

The Gilberts lived in a squalid little flat near the Pantheon where their only running water was a tap on the landing. Stephen had fantasy ideas about shiny metallic houses to be built on top of hills. His heroic wife kept them by factory work (sorting needles is one I remember). They were very kind to me, feeding me an omelette and salad on most evenings that I was there, and we played gentle card games.

Other people were also very kind to me. I was given theatre tickets and saw the great Jean-Louis Barrault, and concert tickets to a piano recital by Poulenc and tickets to the French Open tennis championships, where on a golden sunny afternoon in the Stade Roland Garros I fell in love with the golden girl of tennis, Darlene Hard, then a laughing teenager with a bouncing pony tail. I must have been feeling very susceptible because I was also passionate about Greta Garbo, whom I saw in the film *Queen Christina* in the little cinema which had been the Chinese Embassy and which was decorated with red and gold dragons. The Louvre was free on Mondays in those days so I became very familiar with its long gallery with pictures of martyred saints, the *Mona Lisa*, *Virgin of the Rocks* and heroic paintings by David and Delacroix. I also went to an all-night ball at the École Normale where Adrien was studying and made tentative and clumsy attempts to jive – but it was much more agreeable than the embarrassments of school dances.

At the end of June I went home to England having shed my puppy-fat (no doubt my enforced diet in Paris had helped despite my weekly treat of a coffee meringue or rum baba from the local patisserie) and felt much more grown up and self-confident. With a certificate in French from the Sorbonne (where I had learnt the pleasure of studying hard) I had to some extent overcome the trauma of failing to go to university.

6

BETHNAL GREEN

In the autumn of 1955, aged nineteen, I went to live in a settlement, St Hilda's, in Bethnal Green (in the late nineteenth century young students came from the older universities to do 'good works' in the East End of London – hence settlements such as Oxford House, St Hugh's and St Hilda's). Aunt Saintie, who had made the disparaging remarks about the police service quoted in the prologue, had the idea of weaning me off my intention of joining a working-class occupation and encouraging me into some more middle-class form of social work. She had been one of the earliest mental health workers, employed by the London County Council and later by the Elfrida Rathbone Association.

Bethnal Green had been relatively untouched by wartime bombing so most of the buildings were rather seedy and run-down Victorian houses and workers' dwellings, and there were a few council estates built by the LCC between the wars. St Hilda's was at the western end, not far from Liverpool Street station. I made the naive mistake early on of hanging my pants to dry on the flat roof outside my bedroom only to find them covered in great greasy smuts from the steam engines. The twenty or so residents of St Hilda's were all young women working locally as librarians or secretaries, and I remember the excitement of being introduced to the first of the James Bond books by them.

The settlement ran various youth clubs, where, as a shy and rather awkward teenager, I found it embarrassingly difficult to talk to the boys and girls. Once a week I worked in the Citizens Advice Bureau and one day a week I went out with Meals on Wheels in Shoreditch. Both of these revealed levels of misery and deprivation that were deeply depressing and hardened my resolve not to be too intimately involved in other people's lives. It seemed that the responsibilities of the police service would be more short term and adventurous, and would not require me to feel so much of other people's pain and despair.

In the days before the existence of statutory social workers, the Citizens Advice Bureau acted as a clearing house for people whose homes had been destroyed by fire, people who had been evicted, and women who had been assaulted by their husbands or boyfriends. I was made to distinguish between statutory authorities, like the borough council, and their responsibilities and the more flexible help that could be offered by charities and other voluntary organisations.

I found doing Meals on Wheels even more distressing than the short-term crises dealt with by the Citizens Advice Bureau because it exposed me to the long-term misery of some people's lives. We collected unappetizing meals from a local cafeteria and delivered them to solitary people living in often squalid conditions, like one old woman who was desperate to talk and used various excuses to detain us such as the need to change a lightbulb. I particularly remember the horror of one man alone in a nicotine-stained room with no furniture except a bed with sheets that were uniformly brown. He said not a word and just gestured to me to put the tray on a bedside table and I hurriedly escaped.

I can remember a charity supported by St Hilda's called the Children's Country Holiday Fund, which gave people paying small weekly amounts the opportunity to send their children away on holiday. St Hilda's had a list of those who had begun paying but had lapsed and I was sent out one morning to discover what had happened to some of those children. There were two sets of flats in Bethnal Green which had been built at the behest of Baroness Burdett (Money-)Coutts. One was a grim block with deliberately ill-fitting doors and windows because the architect believed in fresh air and said that you cannot trust 'the poor' not to block up ventilators. The other set of dwellings was an extraordinary white mock-Gothic creation with pointed windows and crocketed pinnacles that has since been listed. It was in the latter that I found the mother and children I sought in a dark dungeon lit only by candles because the electricity had been cut off. I was very shocked and went to see the Housing Department, who were unable to assist and where for the only time in my life I fainted.

On another occasion in September I went with the woman who ran St Hilda's, a stocky, rather masculine woman we knew as Miss Bright, and a group of the children on a day's outing to Kent where some philanthropic but misguided people had offered them hospitality. Many of the children had never been on a train before or seen fields and cows. When we arrived at the house the children went wild – running about in uncontrollable excitement, taking their clothes off and jumping in and out of the small fish pond.

It was a warm day. I took some of them away to pick blackberries but the paper bags soon became sodden with blackberry juice and were used as impromptu water bombs to hurl at each other. It was generally rather an exhausted and purple-stained group that we took back to London. One small girl refused to get on a bus outside the Bank of England and lay on the pavement screaming hysterically. She insisted on walking all the way home, and poor Miss Bright had to follow her.

At the end of my time at St Hilda's I spent five weeks in the spring of 1956 working at Bourne and Hollingsworth's department store in New Oxford Street. I was on the counter that sold knitting and embroidery wools, and despite my total ignorance found myself being asked advice about knitting patterns. I rapidly discovered that I was not suited to this job – one woman complained about my insolence when I thought I had been particularly helpful (perhaps I was not subservient enough) and I always seemed to get the till and change wrong. As usual, I did not feel comfortable in the role and was horrified to find one day that I was being paid more than one of the long-established women.

At Easter I was invited to join the Bedales sailing trip on the Broads and had a lovely time. We had three boats and slept on board and washed in river water. I learnt a little about sailing and quanting and heard a bittern boom. At the end of May that year I set off with my parents and my brother, Tom, to drive to Istanbul. I had recently passed my driving test at the second attempt, so was to take part in the driving. The journey was to take two weeks and was an adventure in itself.

On that first trip to Istanbul we stopped for a day here and there. We stayed two nights on the shores of a tree-fringed Austrian lake amidst pine trees where I loved the painted furniture, and we also stopped at Sarajevo, with its echoes of 1914. My most recent visit to Sarajevo, in 2018 with the House of Lords International Relations Committee, showed me a war-torn town which filled me with sadness. Dubrovnik provided convents whose restful shade contrasted with the dazzling marble of the main street. Altogether it was a journey of contrasts between the forests of Germany and the bare hills studded with prickly scarlet-flowered pomegranate bushes of southern Europe, between the decaying holy city of Peć and the brutal, concrete-reinforced streets of Titograd (now Podgorica).

We first stayed with diplomatic friends in Brussels, and then in the Saar with Austrians my mother had known before the war. In southern Germany we spent a night at an inn where I encountered a duvet for the first time, and in Austria we stayed two nights at a smart lakeside resort. The adventure began when we reached Yugoslavia, where the roads deteriorated sharply – often they were unmetalled and full of potholes. Cars were so rare that tortoises had time to cross the road and in villages we were pursued by shouting children and fierce barking dogs. In Ljubljana (now in Slovenia, and a holiday destination for hikers and wildflower enthusiasts) we stopped for petrol, which was brought in a watering can out of sort of stone sepulchre in a cave in the hillside. We spent nights in Zagreb, where I became slightly drunk on sweet white wine, and in Sarajevo, then a city with a skyline of minarets surrounded by open countryside where we were met on arrival by a pond full of croaking frogs in the twilight.

My mother was very keen to revisit Dubrovnik, where she had spent six weeks in the 1930s when her mother, Pau-pau, was ill with typhoid, so we deviated from the direct route onto even poorer roads. Dubrovnik was unforgettably lovely and still is despite the hordes of tourists. We stayed in a hotel to the south of the city with its great battlemented encircling walls. The hotel had its own pier jutting into the pellucid sea full of fish swimming as though in an aquarium. The great marble central street shone blindingly in the bright sunlight and in the evening flocks of swifts screamed up and down. There were of course no other tourists in the lovely small cloisters, and the woman managing our hotel muttered about Tito's regime. Our only problem was my brother's refusal to eat anything but wiener schnitzels!

After two nights in Dubrovnik in 80-degree temperatures, we climbed up and up from sea level into the mountains of Montenegro, where there were still swathes of snow in the fields. There we stayed in Titograd, then a soulless, newly built city of square concrete blocks which contrasted oddly the following day with the holy city of Peć, which atheistic officialdom had clearly deliberately allowed to decay, although we passed through herds of bleating sheep and goats on their way to be blessed at a holy festival in the town – so there were still local believers.

At the border crossing into Greece we ran into serious problems as we had overstayed our seven-day visas by one day. Discussions had to be conducted in German and they kept on insisting that we should return to Titograd to get our visas renewed. Eventually, after much argument, they were amused to find that my father's job in Istanbul was to be as a passport and visa-control officer (his cover as an MI6 officer) and they let us through the border. Extraordinarily, we now found ourselves on smooth, well-engineered metal roads paid for by the USA as part of their Cold War strategy. We made very good time to the Turkish border at Edirne (Adrianople), where we were met by a member of the British Embassy staff and stayed that first night in Turkey in a hotel, sleeping together in a communal family room with very rudimentary washing facilities down the corridor.

The next day we arrived in Istanbul, where I was to spend the next three months.

7

ISTANBUL

My memories of Istanbul are overlaid by later visits like a palimpsest where the rather shabby streets and crumbling wooden houses are now replaced with shiny tower blocks and through-routes filled with swirling traffic. In 1956 there were no bridges across the Bosporus while there are now two linking Europe with Asia – a third is planned. It seemed a much more decisive step when we had to cross the water by one of the ferries which constantly plied up and down, zigzagging between the shores.

That first summer my parents hired a house out at Bebek, which was then an undeveloped suburb to the east of Istanbul. It had wide balconies and was cool in the summer heat, surrounded by scrubby grass where grasshoppers and praying mantises lurked. We had a nightwatchman who sat on the steps leading up to the house. One night he fell asleep, had a nightmare and fell off the steps screaming. Most days we went into the city. I often drove, which as a rather introverted twenty-year-old gave me a sense of empowerment, except on one occasion when I went up a one-way street in the wrong direction and met a tram coming the other way. Traffic was light, and a woman driver was sufficiently unusual to ensure that other drivers gave me a wide berth. The main street leading from the British Consulate to Taksim Square (the centre of the most recent protests against the government) was then a street of brothels with patient lines of men waiting on the pavements. On the opposite pavement was a shop selling Istanbul's best Turkish delight.

We usually parked at the British Consulate – a splendid neoclassical building which had been the embassy at the beginning of the twentieth century when the Ottoman Empire still existed. Such casual parking would now be impossible; since it was bombed in the 1990s it has been guarded by tall security fences and a fortified entrance. In the building my father had two separate offices with separate staff – one for his cover job as a visa control officer and one for his secret service role. We never heard anything about either job, except the occasional muttering from my father about British travellers whose motorbikes had broken down and who expected to be repatriated without cost – a consequence of the city being on the Beatnik trail to India. Whilst my father was working, we would often take a ride in a dolmuş (a word meaning 'full up' – a sort of communal taxi) across the Golden Horn to the old city with its wonderful skyline of domes and minarets and the high arches of the Roman aqueduct. We wandered around the old buildings and spent many happy hours in the covered market drinking little glasses of tea and bargaining half-heartedly over rugs. My mother bought kelims and soft rugs of woven hair from Angora goats in natural shades of black, brown and white which still smelt strongly goatish. I had two which lasted for many years. My mother also later began to collect old folk embroideries with pastel and silver threads on unbleached linen.

Of course we visited the buildings that are now tourist sights and which I have visited since so it is difficult to untangle the memories. The dusty arena in front of the great sixth-century Hagia Sophia, where Greek and Roman chariot races were once held, is now a smart paved piazza with ice cream carts, restaurants and long queues for the ticket booths. Now that Turkey has a thriving economy people are no longer bothered by moneychangers offering three times the official rate of exchange. Lavatories are now usable. Otherwise much is as it has been for centuries – the Hagia Sophia is still mysteriously exhilarating, the capitals of its marble columns are still like frozen lace, and some lovely mosaics (including a melancholy twelfth-century Christ) have now been uncovered on the first floor. The rambling Topkapı Palace continues to astonish, and the sixteenth-century mosque of Suleiman the Magnificent, the Süleymaniye (the masterpiece of his great architect, Sinan), is for me a supreme space for tranquil meditation.

Our social life seemed to consist of an endless and exquisitely boring round of cocktail parties, each with a regular cast of British colleagues and a sprinkling of Turks. These occasions were apparently an important part of my father's secret service role – what would now be called 'networking'. At one, I was lustfully kissed by an employee of the British American Tobacco Company – I chiefly remember the unpleasantness of his bristly moustache. We also went swimming in the freezing waters of the Bosporus and I was horribly sunburnt one afternoon spent sitting by the warmer waters of the Sea of Marmara. My skin peeled as never before or since. My parents gradually made friends outside the diplomatic circles. There was Yildiz, a distinguished woman photographer (my brother, who stayed on in Istanbul, claims that my father later had an affair with her), and Aliye Berger, a painter.

One day we went to the Asian side to visit an old Turkish lady living in one of the lovely old pale wooden palaces, the haveli, right on the edge of the rushing waters of the Bosporus that swirled round the point of land outside her house. We were served small cups of tea with a teaspoonful of jam in a saucer alongside as we sat in her cool and elegant sitting room set about with embroidered cushions. In Istanbul there was also a community of British expats whose families had been trading in Istanbul for the past century – a curiously faded remnant of what must once have been an energetic entrepreneurial community. However, as usual, my parents seemed to fit in better with the artistic community than with our fellow compatriots.

Istanbul then was a thoroughly cosmopolitan city of many faiths and nationalities so we excited little interest. Turkey's neutral status during the Second World War meant that it had been a hotbed of spies and contacts between opposing nations, and some of that atmosphere still persisted. I have been astonished on visits to Istanbul fifty years later (most recently in 2016 for a conference when I had the pleasure of acting as a tour guide for Alf Dubbs, taking him to some of my favourite mosques, and in 2017 and 2018 for election monitoring) by the increasing Islamification, the number of women wearing headscarves, the rise of Turkish nationalism and the hostility in some quarters to Ataturk, the father of the nation.

After three happy but idle months in Istanbul I returned to England to apply for the Metropolitan Police. I had been unable to imagine myself in any sort of job so had not given serious thought to any other occupation, but I thought it would at least be an adventure. I had the feeling that life would now be serious and no longer much fun, but with curious self-confidence I had no doubt that I would cope. Whilst waiting I lived with my father's sister, my godmother Aunt Judy and her family – Uncle Gerald and their three small boys, David, Paul and Ben. I was to stay there a lot during the four years that my parents were away, and I still sometimes have a lunch around Christmas with David and Paul.

8

RECRUIT

Shortly after my return from Istanbul in the autumn of 1956 I had two days of IQ tests and interviews for the Met. We stayed overnight in a bleak little building in Beak Street near Oxford Circus, sleeping in cubicles on hard bunkbeds between wooden partitions. I remember nothing about the interviews but wrote an essay proving conclusively that it was impossible for a manned space rocket to return safely from the moon. We were also weighed and measured, had our teeth examined and our eyes tested. People often fail the eye tests, especially men, because of colour blindness and the resulting inability to read traffic lights. I was accepted as a new recruit.

I arrived at Peel House in Regency Street on 19 November 1956. Of our monthly intake of forty recruits, half the men were sent to the Metropolitan Police Training Complex at Hendon (where I was later to be the Commander) and the other half of the men including us six women were to be at Peel House, which was a grim Victorian building of concrete and iron staircases. The men were residential but we were bussed in each day from our lodgings,

Peto House (named after the first woman superintendent) near Baker Street, which were ruled over by Sergeant Saville, who had a voice like a sergeant major, so we did not dare misbehave.

There were 300 women in the Met at that time and about 19,000 men. As we were seen as specialists in matters relating to women and children we had a separate hierarchy, with Superintendent Bather at its peak. Nowadays the Met has nearly 30,000 officers of whom about a quarter are women. This overall increase in force strength is more apparent than real as in the 1950s all officers worked a six-day week with an extra day a month for which we were paid overtime, whereas now that the five-day week is the norm it takes more officers to cover the twenty-four-hour cycle.

We were sworn in on that first day and I was allotted 1517 as my warrant number, meaning that 1516 women had joined the Met before me since the time that women had become sworn officers in 1920, after the passage of the Sex Disqualification (Removal) Act 1919. My shoulder number, in the days before name badges, was 192, which I was to carry for the next five years. When I became a sergeant it became 13, which I was told had belonged to a notoriously unpopular predecessor, Sergeant Hook.

We were all issued with the solid black 'Instruction Book' and our classes consisted of a great deal of rote learning of passages from the book and of powers of arrest and the obligatory recitation of the so-called 'Primary Objects' – 'The Primary Object of an efficient police force is the prevention of crime, the next the detection and apprehension of offenders...' It was said that this had been written personally by Sir Richard Mayne, one of the two first Commissioners of the Met, but some research I did many years later showed that there were several different versions drafted by civil servants in the Home Office.

We also had to pass a first-aid exam and had some rudimentary self-defence training (I tried to put a half-nelson on Uncle Gerard but failed utterly). There were swimming lessons for those officers who could not swim. On numerous occasions, regardless of the weather, we gathered in the chilly yard for practical exercises dealing with arrests and traffic accidents. Even then we were expected to ask rote questions, often aided by mnemonics. That for traffic accidents was COW – Casualties, Obstruction, Witnesses – and the first question to be asked on arrival at the scene was, 'Did anyone see what happened?'

Each morning we paraded in the yard with the other classes and were expected to line up in neat rows for inspection. Our right marker (a military expression meaning the officer who stood at the right-hand end of the line) was 'Taffy' Jones, who had been in the Welsh Guards and was very smart but had a high-pitched treble voice which caused much amusement to the other classes when he shouted 'right turn' and 'dismiss'. We also had to march to the public swimming pool in Buckingham Palace Road in full uniform and I always had difficulty keeping in step. Fortunately it was never a skill that I ever had to use again. Occasionally there were lighter moments. At Christmas we had a show and I learnt all the traditional music hall songs like 'My Old Man's a Dustman' and 'Doing the Lambeth Walk'.

For the first weeks we women were without full uniforms as our skirts and jackets were made to measure by a small tailor's shop on Ludgate Hill. We had been issued with shoes and hats and overcoats and shirts like the men, although our shirts were white not blue. Our shirts had detachable collars which had to be sent each week to a laundry to be starched. As the collars frayed they developed saw-like edges which rubbed my neck sore.

Fortunately, after a couple of years they were replaced with more sensible collared shirts. We also had to learn how to quite literally spit and polish our shoes with saliva and black shoe polish and little circular movements of the cloth. I did not enjoy my time at Peel House but we, including the men, were all suffering together and I found the learning of great chunks of the Instruction Book rather easier than did some others. Moreover, there was a sense of shared camaraderie in our common suffering.

The training at Peel House was under the control of Chief Superintendent Tommy Wall, who, although a member of the Salvation Army, was a blustering bully and much feared. He would come in to the classroom and pick on the most nervous recruit. In our class we had a young man who stammered and it was he who was picked on to repeatedly recite the 'Primary Objects'. I felt embarrassed and saddened. Tommy Wall excused himself on the grounds that it was an unkind world outside and that he was just toughening us up. I could not see that being abused by our colleagues would help us to deal with public insults or violence.

Some years later, when I was responsible for some of the arrangements for the International Police Boxing and Wrestling Championships, there was a line of reserved seats in the front row. Tommy Wall came up to me and asked if one was for him. I said, 'They are only for the Very Important People, Sir.' He was furious and stalked off, later sending his Staff Officer to tell me off for being impertinent – but it was worth it.

9

STEPNEY

I arrived at Leman Street Police Station in Stepney on the borders of the City of London on a cold dark day in February 1957. I had lived in Greece as a child and in France and Turkey, but Stepney then seemed to me as alien and exciting as a foreign country – its past is now obliterated by the overspill of large office blocks from the City of London. The bombing raids on the London Docks had still left great, wide-open muddy spaces where the meths drinkers huddled round makeshift fires. The men (mostly ex-servicemen) were sometimes joined in drunken choruses by one or two pathetic women. On a cold, wet Christmas Eve I 'arrested' for his own safety a meths drinker who was lying in a puddle of rainwater singing 'Oh Come All Ye Faithful', and he spent a warm dry night in the police station.

The main streets were still paved with slippery brick-shaped granite setts which were lethal in wet weather, and the trolleybuses still ran in Commercial Road, causing serious traffic jams when their poles came off the overhead wires. In the evening every street corner on the Commercial Road was occupied by a prostitute, many of whom we got to know well, and I became used to seeing discarded condoms lying in the gutters. Outside the many pubs – one on every street corner – late on Saturday evenings there would often be brawling groups of drunken men who usually melted way at the sight of a police uniform – I was advised always to approach slowly. This was of course well before the advent of personal radios and fast response cars.

Over much of the shattered landscape of what had been small terraced houses presided the great skeletal towers of Hawksmoor's St George's-in-the-East, like a ghostly white ship in a sea of self-sown willow herb and buddleias growing in the ruined lumps of the stone walls. Near the police station were the alleyways where Jack the Ripper committed his murders. I also recall certain smells, the acrid urine stench of unwashed children, the aroma of drunken adults, the curious musty smell of a young woman I took to be deloused at a cleansing station, and always the smell of kippers in hallways. The year that I was on night duty over Christmas the men brought me some jellied eels from Tubby Isaac's aromatic stall in the Whitechapel Road to try along with their homemade potato wine. Down at the empty bonded warehouses by London Dock there were still faint scents of cinnamon and nutmeg that were ghostly relics of the spice trade. Some more rural smells were produced by the few remaining brewery dray horses.

It was a place in transition – still mostly run-down streets of decaying terrace houses with some replacement council flats. The contemporary television series *Call the Midwife*, based at the other end of Stepney, gives a realistic picture of the poverty of the area. Some remaining Victorian tenements had grey concrete stairs with iron railings and large notices saying 'Do Not Spit' on the landings. The population of the western end of Stepney still contained the remnants of an earlier population of Jewish refugees, most of whom had moved to other parts of London, but chickens were slaughtered in the kosher manner in one of the street markets and some of the elderly population spoke only Yiddish. One important relic of the flourishing Jewish population was Bloom's delicatessen in Whitechapel Road, where we bought delicious late-night snacks.

The other distinctive members of the population that we dealt with were the Maltese who ran the network of sleazy little cafes in Cable Street and Christian Street that were a magnet for young girls who had run away from troubled homes. Many of the girls ended up there and were exploited as prostitutes. Rather than fists the Maltese used knives in their fights, which was seen as unsporting and un-British. How things have changed.

At Leman Street the policewomen's offices were in a semi-basement below the prisoners' cells. These sometimes leaked, and sinister stains appeared on our ceilings. There were fifteen policewomen including an inspector, Miss Derwin, and two sergeants. We twelve constables were divided into an early and a late shift. Curiously we worked seven-and-a-half-hour shifts and had an hour for lunch because we had 90 per cent of the men's pay (they worked eight-hour shifts and had three-quarters of an hour for lunch). I resented the assumption that we were not able to work a full tour of duty.

The most memorable of the two sergeants was Rosemary Botherway, who was a fantasist given to relating dramatic and distorted versions of events. She lived with a chronically ill and disabled mother, so perhaps needed to escape from reality. She disliked one of my fellow officers, and late in 1958 told a wholly fallacious account of what this officer had done when they arrested a man for being drunk and disorderly. She submitted a report denigrating the officer to the woman superintendent at the Area HQ, Miss Sidell, who was responsible for all the women in North East London. As I had been a witness to part of the incident, in some trepidation and feeling like a sneak, I went to see Miss Sidell but she received me kindly and with understanding as presumably she knew Sergeant Botherway well. There were no apparent repercussions, but shortly afterwards, at the end of my two years' probation, in 1959 I was transferred to Kings Cross.

As Miss Sidell ran the women's cricket team, where I was a stonewall bat and occasional wicket-keeper, I later came to know her better and admired her calm good humour. We were very bad at cricket, losing to all the serious women's teams in the Home Counties, but we enjoyed ourselves. I also remember one delightful occasion when the women's cricket team were on our way to play the policewomen in Leeds and stopped en route for a picnic (this was before the advent of motorways and service stations) and I amused Miss Sidell and Denise de Vitre (from the Home Office) by cooling our bottles of wine in a nearby stream. This was one of the rare occasions when I felt able to be my frivolous self. As a police officer I was expected to be calm and controlled, and I have never been good at being part of a group. My peripatetic early life meant that I was always an outsider at the schools I attended, and I felt even more isolated by being with people who had no interest in art or literature, although there was the camaraderie of shared experiences. The fact that I was gay should not have been a bar to closer ties, and there was a substantial lesbian subculture among the policewomen, but I was never part of that scene and sex was never overtly discussed. However, I knew which women were living with other women.

I remember some of the policewomen at Leman Street as being great characters. There was Jeff (Jennifer) Robinson, a Cambridge graduate who drove a Morgan sports car and was a chain smoker. She predicted that I would take up smoking when I encountered my first dead body but I never did. Megan Brown was Welsh and an ex-prison officer who had a great gift, born perhaps of experience, for knowing when a young girl was telling lies. I naively tended to believe everyone at first but gradually learnt that if a girl said all her relations were dead, or could not remember her birthday, that there were grounds for suspicion. Megan had great tenacity and dedication. One evening as she was coming off duty late in the evening someone in passing muttered, '57' to her. Most people would have ignored this fragment of information but she knew that 57 Fieldgate Street was the homeless men's hostel and immediately turned round, went there and found a very young girl being concealed by one of the men. I was full of admiration for her dedication and acumen.

There were no statutory social workers in the community then. Children's Officers were only responsible for children actually in the care of the local council. The two statutory organisations that dealt with 'problem' families and neglected, missing or ill-treated children were the police service and the NSPCC. We alone had the power in an emergency to remove children from their families and take them before a juvenile court. There were of course a number of non-statutory groups like the Quakers and Church Army who did astonishing work with families. It is a sad fact that social workers are now presumed to be responsible for everything, so they always make convenient scapegoats when things go wrong.

After our initial thirteen weeks at the training complex, and during our two years on probation, we had a weekly class at

Arbour Square, the Divisional Headquarters, but policewomen had an additional five weeks of classes – two weeks during our first year and three weeks at the end of our probation. We learnt the laws on neglect and cruelty to children and what signs to look out for when there was an allegation – 'always strip the child to see if there are any bruises' and 'look in the larder to see if there is food in the house'. We also were instructed on the taking of statements about rape or indecent exposure and shown a grainy brown film of childbirth, and advised on the materials used by abortionists such as 'slippery elm' and knitting needles. Fortunately, abortion was legalised not long afterwards and deaths and injuries from backstreet abortions sharply decreased. On our second course we visited an open prison and sat in a court at the Old Bailey where I heard Christmas Humphreys successfully defend a young murderer whose conviction was downgraded to manslaughter.

Despite our specialist status at Leman Street we were assigned to beats and expected to patrol them and deal with any incident that arose. Our specialist status and extra training meant that male officers were reliant upon us to deal with problem families, young girls, children and sex offences so we were treated with respect and little sexism. Most policemen then were older married men and many had seen wartime service. After a brief few weeks of patrolling with another policewoman, Betty, who did not speak to me and gave me hand signals when about to turn a corner, I was on my own and very nervous to begin with – every scream or trail of blood on the pavement made me fear a homicide. We all worked a six-day week, although one day a fortnight was on overtime and our pay after deductions was less than £6 a week. We did get free accommodation, on the other hand. Our main task in patrolling the streets was to look for young girls missing from home as well as more general tasks such as parking offences, public disorder and lost dogs. If lost dogs were a nuisance – barking too much – the Station Officer would surreptitiously let them loose again.

In the days before the Street Offences Act, which drove prostitution underground or into the backstreets, there were three main centres in London: Praed Street near Paddington Station, the West End and Stepney. In the evenings there were prostitutes, called 'Toms' by the male officers, on every street corner near Gardiner's Corner at their regular stations. Many of them were respectable middle-aged women such as blonde Nellie Currie (whose daughter was a nurse) and the perpetually tipsy Annie Brown. They were arrested on what was effectively a rota (being fined £2 at Thames Magistrates Court and let out the next day), and we had to look after them at the police station. They complained bitterly if they felt it was not their turn on the rota and that they were being arrested too often!

The offence was 'soliciting to the annoyance', and the arresting officers invented annoyed passers-by, but I could never bring myself to join in this charade. There was undoubtedly general annoyance to the local residents and to respectable women who resented being mistaken for prostitutes, and so the police service had to appear to be responding to public opinion, however ineffectively. The 150 or so regular prostitutes were often our best source of information about what they called 'mysteries' – new young girls who appeared on the streets or in the cafes – possibly out of altruism, possibly because they did not want young rivals on the streets.

The girls who did turn up in the area were often lured into prostitution through the aforementioned network of Maltese-run cafes around Cable Street. They had allegedly learnt their trade by catering to the needs of British sailors in Malta. St Katherine's and London Dock had long since closed but the ghosts of mariners still lingered around the Union Jack Club in Dock Street and the long-term association between Malta and the Royal Navy. A major part of our work was to identify girls who were under seventeen and return them to their families. We should certainly have done more to find out why they were reluctant to return home, but as there were no social workers to deal with family issues there was little we could do about their backgrounds. When it came to the 'problem' families who lived in our area, however, we kept a 'story book' in which we recorded our regular encounters with them and did our best to help. One woman who was regularly reported as missing by her sad little Asian husband (who allegedly had bite marks all over his back) was sent on a three-month residential course on home management by the Quakers and returned totally transformed as a model wife and mother.

We always did our best to open the young girls' eyes to the cynical exploitation that was going on – they believed that their recently acquired Maltese boyfriend was genuinely in love with them, only to find that they were expected to earn their keep. One of my fellow probationers (a committed Christian and even more naïve than I) embarrassingly gave them moral lectures about sin. I particularly remember one attractive and intelligent young woman whom we had earnestly tried to dissuade from going with her Maltese boyfriend; she turned up at the police station two weeks later with a badly bruised and swollen face. He had beaten her because she would not go on the streets.

I was very bad at recognising new faces (embarrassingly I stopped and spoke to one girl two nights running and did not recognise her because she had changed her hairstyle – she was annoyed).

I preferred to police the less demanding but historically interesting streets of Wapping or round the Tower of London where the only problems were the questions of tourists and the astonishment of the occasional American that we did not carry guns. Tower Hill was moreover a place of entertainment. Like Hyde Park Corner it was where free speech was allowed, so there were political and religious speeches to listen to, and the occasional escapologist, musician or juggler. Wapping was an eerie place with almost no people living there except some Hungarian refugees who were housed in an old hospital. Lofty empty warehouses towered above the canyon that was Wapping High Street as I made my way to the Thames River Police Station where I sometimes secured an illicit boat ride. The Thames Police have a proud tradition as they were established many years before the Metropolitan Police when the Thames was London's main highway and rife with thieves and smugglers. Most of the officers were ex-Royal Navy and the station had fascinating wall charts of knots and signal flags. Next to the police station was the small park on whose river frontage felons were chained by the neck until three high tides had passed, at which point they were either drowned or released. That area, including the council flats called Stephen and Matilda, is now crowded with hotels and smart housing developments.

After dark we generally patrolled in pairs, which was comforting, but in the absence of personal radios any need for back-up or an ambulance or fire engine meant finding a public phone or a Doctor Who-type police box – I only remember one in our area in Whitechapel Road which could provide a rather cramped refuge from the rain. Our instructions were to give three short blasts on our whistles if we needed help, but that was totally ineffective – as proved by one of my male colleagues who blew his frantically just outside the police station while struggling with a prisoner; nobody came to help. More tragically, two women officers were unable to prevent a very large and heavy man in a house in Cable Street from murdering his wife by jumping up and down on her. They could not restrain him and could not leave to seek help.

On our late evening patrols we encountered both comedy and tragedy. A Missing Persons message had been circulated by teleprinter describing a girl as wearing 'Rock and Roll' stockings. Speculating about what these might be as we walked on the bomb site off Commercial Road, to our astonishment, there in front of us was a young girl with 'Rock' on one calf and 'Roll' on the other; she was safely returned to her parents. Other encounters on that bomb site were less amusing. One dark night we spoke to a heavily pregnant woman of limited intelligence (what we would have then called 'mentally defective'). Two months later she was charged with infanticide. She had given birth in a derelict building and the baby had possibly been strangled by its umbilical cord. She was arrested and detained in hospital, where we served shifts guarding her. She was eventually placed on probation. One of my most awful experiences was sitting for some hours in a grubby flat with a woman in labour who knew the baby was already dead. In those days we could only call ambulances to accidents, not illness in a home, but eventually a male officer used his initiative, rang for an ambulance and said the woman had fallen and so we were relieved of our awful vigil.

There was a great sense of camaraderie at Leman Street – we were policing in a very poor and violent part of London but we were also the twenty-four hour service that people turned to when they were in need, destitute or homeless. There was a generally understood ethos of rough justice. Anyone who assaulted a police officer would be beaten in return and neither would refer to their bruises at court the next day. However, there were dark rumours of unprovoked assaults in the CID offices. The CID were a very separate entity and DIs (detective inspectors) were revered as gods. Even when I formally outranked them I still felt they were my superiors. I saw few examples of violence towards prisoners. On one occasion I saw the station sergeant hit a drunken man on his shins with his truncheon because he would not stop shouting. On another occasion several of us tried to restrain a struggling and deranged woman as we were trying to keep a dressing on her serious scalp wound. When the ambulance men arrived they put a straitjacket on her – the only time I saw one being used.

Stranded people were often given their fare home or allowed to spend a night sleeping in the cells. In emergencies, if people were evicted or there was a house fire, we acted as liaison with charities and the statutory authorities. Some of my most harrowing experiences were dealing with the mentally ill – an elderly and manic Jewish woman who in fevered ramblings said that Winston Churchill would come and save her, others who thought their confused minds were due to the Devil or the neighbour's machinery or to alien radio waves or poisoned cigarettes. Having a great regard for rationality I found these delusions deeply disturbing. I remain disturbed still by the memory of one young and perfectly sane young girl who had been certified as a 'moral defective' (a category that no longer exists) and confined in a mental hospital because of her sexual behaviour. Escorting these women meant that I was already familiar with many of London's mental hospitals before my sister Susie some three or four years later developed schizophrenia with paranoid delusions. One painful result of her illness was that I could no longer talk about my home life and retreated further from personal relationships.

For two Christmases I was the night duty policewoman for the whole division, which encompassed Poplar, Limehouse and Bethnal Green as well as Stepney; it is now called Tower Hamlets. On Christmas Eve 1957 I saw the chaos that was the Accident and Emergency Unit at the London Hospital where the whole reception area was heaving with disorderly drunks, alcohol and blood.

A regular commitment for us as policewomen was the school crossing in Cable Street (famous for the 1930s battle against Oswald Moseley's Blackshirts). It was a shabby street of terraced houses backing on to the raised railway line. On the corner opposite the school crossing there was a breakers' yard guarded by terrifying and fierce Alsatian dogs whose owner was a major receiver of stolen goods. There were always incidents as we worked the crossing, ranging from traffic accidents – a man was hit on the forehead by the wing mirror of a passing lorry and bled copiously – to a complaint about the smells from a neighbour cooking curry.

Most of my arrests during that first two years were for drunkenness or minor thefts, but I did have one for 'Drunk in Charge' one evening on finding a man trying unsuccessfully to unlock his car door and staggering back against a lamp post. He was very drunk and when I said I was arresting him he gallantly said could he walk me home. He pleaded guilty at court and I felt very sorry for him as his business was failing and the resulting twelve-month suspension from driving was the ultimate disaster. I also made one unlawful arrest. One dark evening I was standing in the Commercial Road talking to a male sergeant ('idling and gossiping' as our ex-military officers called it) when he suddenly said, 'Arrest that man.' I turned to see a man urinating copiously but quite discreetly against the wall of a dark alley behind me. I went up to him and said, 'I am arresting you for being drunk and indecent.' He was a very courteous black American and made no protest. To my dismay, I realised that he was not at all drunk. However, he pleaded guilty at Thames Magistrates Court the next day and was fined a notional amount.

Occasionally there would be the excitement of being briefed for a raid on a pub or club where drugs or after-hours drinking were suspected. Despite elaborate precautions against a tip-off, late and secret briefings, much use of blackboard chalk to describe entrances and exits, none of these were successful – we would arrive to find the premises dark and deserted. The only successful raid that I went on was even more farcical. In the days before the Isle of Dogs became the site of the glittering glass and steel towers of Canary Wharf it was an area of traditional two-storied terraced houses inhabited by dockworkers and seamen. The main pub was called the Pride of the Isle, and to encourage trade they had employed an exotic fan dancer. On weekdays she danced half-naked but on Sundays, when the audience was exclusively male (the wives being at home cooking the Sunday roast), she removed her nipple covers and G-string and behind her enormous ostrich-plumed fans she was glimpsed wholly nude. Someone had decided that this constituted a 'Disorderly House', so we raided the pub at considerable expense of time and effort. The magistrates were more sensible and merely bound over the pub to be of good behaviour for twelve months. I enjoyed talking to the fan dancer, who was calm and eminently professional.

One of my more frightening experiences came towards the end of my time at Leman Street in the winter of 1958 when I acted as a decoy for a rapist. A man had indecently assaulted or raped several young women as they got off the bus at the far end of Bethnal Green where he had dragged them onto empty land by the Northern Outfall Sewer. The main description of him was that he wore Wellington boots. For two weeks, armed with a short but heavy CID truncheon tucked up my sleeve, I made several journeys to the end of the bus line where I knew plainclothes officers were lurking in dark doorways. Apart from being kissed in a doorway by one of the officers, nothing more interesting happened during my two weeks. Another team and woman officer took over and they saw and stopped a man wearing Wellington boots who was indeed the rapist.

10

KINGS CROSS

At the end of two fascinating years at Leman Street, which with its wartime ruins and transient population had seemed like a foreign country, at the beginning of 1959 I was transferred to the police station in Kings Cross Road next to Clerkenwell Magistrates Court. Whereas at Leman Street I had been one of fifteen policewomen, some of them fellow cricketers, at Kings Cross I was the only one. It was at times a lonely life, both out on the streets and in the police station. There was one other woman nearby, at Gray's Inn Road Station, but the bulk of the women were at Bow Street, where they were overseen by two women sergeants. One of the sergeants ran a pig farm in Surrey with her partner and got into trouble because we were expected to 'devote our whole time to Police Duties'. Soon after I arrived at Kings Cross I bought my first car, a rather decrepit Morris Minor, and began having the *Guardian* newspaper delivered to the station on a daily basis.

I missed the companionship we had enjoyed at Leman Street, although it was a relief to escape Sergeant Botherway's fantasies.

I had also learnt to change my language and to talk about 'toilets' rather than 'lavatories' (at Bedales it had been called 'the hum') and to realise that 'dinner' occurred at lunchtime and that the evening meal was called 'tea'. Amongst the policewomen at Leman Street there had clearly been a subculture of lesbianism; sex was never mentioned, but it was tacitly understood that several women had permanent female companions. No one made an approach to me, and it was many years later before I had some brief and unsatisfactory flings and one long-term relationship. The remarkable change in the openness of society over recent decades is shown by my cheerfully taking part in a group photograph of gay and lesbian MPs and Peers in 2017.

The only time I heard an overt mention was when the woman sergeant Sylvia King, who had been responsible for new recruits at the training complex, was transferred to an operational front-line role and someone said it was because she had repeatedly seduced young women recruits. She came to live in our section house (accommodation for single officers) in Hackney and she swiftly developed a relationship with another young officer (twenty years her junior). Curiously, I was given a lift by them when I went to stay with my grandmother in Dorset and they were going on to stay in a caravan. They stayed for tea and my grandmother said, perhaps naively, 'What nice girls.' I cannot remember now why I accepted the lift, but I recall that I felt uncomfortable and went back to London by train.

My one particular friendship at Leman Street had been with Joan Coveney. She was also in the cricket team – a large, bouncy girl. One weekend in 1958 she took me on an exciting ride on the back of her Lambretta scooter (no helmets then) to her parents' house in Charlton. We went to watch the local football team play a home match – my first experience of standing on the terraces. In another first, we had winkles for tea, to be extracted with a pin. I had other footballing experiences. When I became a sergeant at East Ham in 1961, it was the glory days for West Ham United as Bobby Moore captained them to a European Cup Winners' Cup, and I became a rather lukewarm supporter of the club. Much later I was the Ch.Supt responsible for policing the crowds at Brentford Football Club.

I spent the night with Joan in a double bed, largely awake and perched on the edge for fear of rolling into her! I was very envious that because she had finished her two years' probation she was able to apply to join the police contingent going out to Cyprus during the 'troubles' there. I was some months short of two years when they asked for volunteers and would have loved to have served in the land of my birth. When she came back two years later, she married a soldier. I went to visit her once in their house in south-east London where she sadly seemed to have lost most of her bounce and joie de vivre. Inappropriately, I took a framed print by Ivon Hitchens as a house-warming present.

There was very little street life around my new station in Kings Cross; the prostitutes around the railway station mostly plied their trade from small, shabby hotels and there were far fewer pubs and consequent street brawls. Some of the prostitutes were young Irish girls who had left school at fourteen and come to London. Liaising with Irish police in an attempt to get them returned home was particularly difficult, and they usually ended up in the care of social services before absconding once more. For many years, until the recent redevelopment and gentrification, the area around the railway station deteriorated further and became a notorious haunt of drug addicts and prostitutes.

Blocks of flats and business premises did not make for interesting patrolling and I was often bored. There were some famous places on the division – Sadler's Wells, the vast Mount Pleasant postal office and the headquarters of the Thames Water Authority based on the free-flowing springs and the Peerless Pools where women bathed in the eighteenth century in diaphanous see-through dresses, but these sites had little relevance for police work. There was more of interest on the borders of the subdivision. At the bottom end, bordering on the City and Smithfield Meat Market, there were the shops selling butchering equipment, great glistening knives and cleavers; at the top end, round the Angel (the old music hall), there was the Chapel Street Market where I once helped to arrest a street bookmaker who did not expect a police officer to be female and had not stopped accepting bets quickly enough. Other forms of gambling in the street, like 'Pitch and Toss', were also illegal until the introduction of betting shops. Like the arrest of prostitutes at Leman Street, the arrest of bookies and street gamblers was a sort of mutually understood game and a tax on their business.

My main human contact was with the probation officers in the court next door, where I perforce spent a lot of time as the magistrates insisted on having a policewoman present when there were women prisoners. Also, once a week I had to sit in the matrimonial court where women sued their husbands for maintenance. I learnt a distressing amount about the traumas of married life. There were also paternity cases (before the advent of DNA testing), with unmarried mothers asking for maintenance from their ex-boyfriends. It is a measure of my naïve romanticism about relationships at the age of twenty-three that I thought these young couples should get married. I was soon made to see sense by the probation officers. I was also amused by a friendship of sorts with one of our male (and married) sergeants, Jimmy Martin, who was lively and flirtatious and kept trying to persuade me that a weekend away with him would be an experience I would not regret. Many years later I was saddened to hear that he had been dismissed on corruption charges while running a crime squad as an inspector.

There were occasional station outings by coach as few people had cars in those days. On one occasion there was a family outing to Brighton Races that was fairly sedate as we were accompanied by the men's wives and children – most of whom were dropped off at the beach. I went on to watch the races on the high bare downland and enjoyed the open air and a small flutter on the horses. Crates of beer were loaded onto the coach for the return journey but I saw no obvious drunkenness. On another occasion we went to Southend to support the police road walkers race. That did seem to be an excuse for stopping at various pubs on both legs of the journey, and we saw little of the race!

About once every two months I would be the night duty policewoman for the whole division and was stationed at Bow Street (opposite the Opera House – the only police station, at the behest of Queen Victoria, to have white lamps outside rather than blue) with its market porters, strong smell of cabbages and pubs open at breakfast time for the night workers. Most of the night was usually spent playing gin rummy for penny points with the permanent night telephonist, the male gaoler and a station sergeant. There was an all-night canteen at Bow Street and I enjoyed having a full English breakfast at two o'clock in the morning. One of the few incidents I remember from this time occurred at Charing Cross Hospital where I saw my first dead body – that of a woman who had died suddenly of a heart attack. She looked quite peaceful but her bewildered husband stood movingly by her side whilst I asked him to sign for the contents of her handbag and pockets. On another occasion I went in the police van with a young and rather bumptious girl who had absconded from one of the large mental hospitals near Epsom. Her only symptom was apparently a settled intention to commit suicide. I was horrified by the behaviour of several of the hospital staff who held her down and forcibly injected her.

One of the most unpleasant police tasks is having to break the news of a sudden death to relatives. One never knows quite what to expect. On one occasion when a woman had cut her throat in a station lavatory I went with a sergeant to break the news to her husband. He was apparently totally unaffected (she had made previous suicide attempts), and when told of the manner of her death he went away to check his cut-throat razors and came back to tell us calmly that one of them was missing. On one occasion I arrested a woman for attempted suicide (a criminal offence until 1961). She had been attempting to throw herself under a bus and was in the casualty department of the Royal Free Hospital. She had also broken a light bulb and attempted to cut her wrists. The doctor in casualty was proposing to discharge her, whereupon she locked herself in the lavatory. Fortunately the policeman I was with managed to force his way in. I formally arrested her and we took her to the police station. I did not notice but he, more observant and experienced, saw her clenched fist and found it full of more shards of glass. She was clearly mentally ill, and I took her to court where eventually, and appropriately, a hospital order was made for her detention in a mental hospital.

One day in the front office a man came to the counter and said, 'I have killed my wife.' He had indeed killed her two days

My father, John Robert Hilton, and mother, 'Peggy' Hilton (née Stephens).

Me as a young child.

My sister Dinah as a young girl.

My sister Susie as a young girl.

My brother Tom in his youth.

Dinah in adulthood.

Susie in a recent picture.

Tom as an adult.

A view of Athens in the 1940s, when we were there, with the Acropolis dominating the landscape.

Me, Dinah and Susie (left to right) posing in front of our smart German car in Greece.

Me, Dinah and Susie on the coast near Piraeus.

The view from our house at Nea Kifissia of Mount Parnes and the mental asylum. Painted by my mother.

Bedales School, where I was a pupil from 1948 to 1954.

The view from my parents' flat in Istanbul, painted by my mother.

The Hagia Sophia in Istanbul in 1960, around the time I was there. (Courtesy of the Dutch Nationaalarchief)

Right: Me, newly promoted to sergeant, in 1961.

Below: Crowd control! I can be seen in the centre, with outstretched arms. The cause of this stir was likely a visit by The Beatles.

Participating in a civil defence exercise.

More crowd control – I can be seen on the right.

Patrolling as an inspector in Chapel Street Market, Islington.

The Whitechapel
Gallery (left), designed
by my great-uncle,
the architect Charles
Harrison Townsend.

Gardiner's Corner, at the
junction of Whitechapel
High Street, Commercial
Street and Leman
Street. Named for
the department store
that once inhabited
the building, it was
a popular location
for prostitutes when
I worked the area.
(© City of London
Corporation)

St George's in the East amid the ruins.

Above: The National Police Staff College at Bramshill House, which I attended both as a student and as a staff member.

Left: Me, newly promoted to the rank of Commander.

Riot gear!

Lord Bramall presenting
me with the Queen's
Police Medal.

Left: Me in India.

Below: Me in Xinjiang, Outer Mongolia.

Dressed for a State opening
of Parliament.

My coat of arms.

My parents' house in Cyprus.

My maternal grandmother's house, 'Crowsnest', where we spent much of the war. It was designed by my father.

'Glebe Cottage', my paternal grandparents' retirement cottage in Dorset.

My painting of 'Hope Cottage', my parents' retirement cottage in Wiltshire.

Above left: Pembroke Scott Stephens (1835–1915), my maternal grandfather.

Above right: My maternal grandmother Pauline Stephens (née Boucher), 'Pau-Pau', with her two sisters, Helen and St. Clair ('Saintie'), either side of her.

Above left: My paternal grandfather, Oscar Hilton/Hildesheim, painted by his wife, Louisa.

Above right: My paternal grandmother, Louisa Hilton (née Holdsworth), 'Granny'.

Left: My maternal great-grandfather, Walter Mallaby Townsend (1848–1905).

Below: My maternal great-grandfather, Pauline Townsend, 'Bonnemaman'.

Bottom left: My great-grandfather's brother Charles Harrison Townsend (1851–1928), a distinguished architect who was responsible for the Whitechapel Gallery, the Horniman Museum and the Bishopsgate Institute.

Bottom right: A more distant ancestor, the violinist and composer Felix Janiewicz (1762–1848).

before by fracturing her skull with one of the heavy rollers from a mangle, and had then apparently tried to electrocute her – there were burn marks on her legs (later in court he was to claim that this was an attempt to revive her after having hit her thinking she was a burglar). He had spent two days driving around with his two small children, a boy and a girl, and took them to the seaside before taking them to his wife's parents, with whom they had regularly stayed, and then he had come into the police station. Part of the trigger for the murder may have been the stress caused by the failure of his business, a shoe shop, but as he never admitted his guilt in court it is unclear what had ultimately provoked the attack. I went round to his flat with a policeman to await the arrival of the CID and the police surgeon. The wife's body was in bed and covered up so there was nothing distressing to see – much to my relief.

However, I was later horrified by the attitude of his mother, who when we visited did not enquire after her grandchildren but said, 'What is going to happen to the car?' I suppose now that this reaction may have been due to shock. The husband subsequently wrote a letter from prison saying that he wanted his children to be with his parents, so I went to the Juvenile Court and obtained an order keeping them with the wife's parents with whom they already had a close relationship and with whom they had always spent their time out of school. He was convicted, but it was odd that neither I nor the station sergeant who had heard his initial confession were called to give evidence. The CID moved in mysterious ways and no doubt wanted the kudos of the arrest and conviction.

In 1960, late in my time at Kings Cross, I was taken on a raid of a smart brothel in Curzon Street because of my ability to speak French. In the late 1950s, one of the most notorious Mafia outfits in London was that of the Messina Brothers, who smuggled drugs and ran brothels. Although they were Italian, their prostitutes, strangely, were Belgian. The brothel was in a very smart, tall (four-storey) building in that elegant part of London. The superintendent leading the raid rang the front doorbell and half a dozen officers piled in when the door was opened. As I entered, the woman who had opened the door shouted up the stairs, '*Therese, les flics, ils font sauter le bordel*! (The cops, they're raiding the brothel!)' – a statement that I was later to relate in evidence at Bow Street Magistrates Court. Whilst other officers searched the premises, I was left with the three mature, well-dressed prostitutes and their maid in their elegant, rather Edwardian first-floor sitting room, furnished with comfortable chairs and fringed lampshades, whilst the half-dressed male clients hurriedly tumbled downstairs and out of the front door. Various pieces of equipment such as whips and canes and handcuffs were collected whilst I continued to eavesdrop on the conversation in French. However, they soon realised that I understood (a poker face not coming naturally to me) and nothing more of interest was said. This brothel was a considerable contrast to the ones in Stepney, which usually consisted of a dingy room shared by two young prostitutes.

During my time at Kings Cross I persuaded the authorities to give me some extra leave and went for a month to visit my parents in Turkey.

11

TURKISH INTERREGNUM

Because I couldn't afford the airfare, I decided to travel to
Istanbul by train – a three-day journey that cost £40 return (this
was the early summer of 1960). Everyone assumes that this was
the luxurious Orient Express of Agatha Christie's crime novel but
it was not like that at all. There was no restaurant car so I had
to provide my own food. I took a whole cooked chicken which
began to smell by the third day, so I disposed of the remaining
half at a wayside station in Yugoslavia. Drinking water came
from taps on the station platforms, and I was nervous as it
was never clear when the train was about to leave. In Germany
and Austria the train was reasonably comfortable and my
fellow travellers were respectable and well-to-do, viewing me
somewhat askance. Once behind the Iron Curtain in Yugoslavia
we transferred to an older and less comfortable train where
I usually had a compartment to myself and could stretch out on
a hard, narrow seat. By this part of the journey it had become a
local train, stopping at small stations, and at one I was joined by
three Yugoslavian peasants who offered me slices of their garlic

sausage and coarse bread for breakfast while I tried to explain with gestures and my school atlas where I was headed.

In Bulgaria we passed through Sofia by night. An old woman was arrested for smuggling a sack full of shoes and bundled off the train. At the border, to my dismay, my passport was taken away and an hour and a half later I was just beginning to panic when a fellow English passenger rushed in agitatedly from the next compartment and said, 'Have they taken your passport too?' This was reassuring, and shortly afterwards our passports were returned.

In Istanbul my parents were no longer living out in the suburbs at Bebek but had a smart flat in the centre of the city with a view of the Bosporus, its ships and oil tankers, and beyond to the Asiatic shore. The plan for the holiday was to drive across Turkey, fly to Cyprus for a few days, return by boat, and then to travel slowly back to Istanbul, camping at night along Turkey's southern shore and up through Ephesus and Bursa and İznik (the original Nicaea of the Nicene Creed) to the Sea of Marmara. Despite sundry mishaps (engine failure, punctures), this, in my parents' by now rather battered old Humber Hawk, we largely achieved.

The worst days were the first and second, on which we should have completed an easy run to stay with friends in Ankara. On the first day, one of the cows grazing by the side of the road under the guidance of a small girl with a stick suddenly decided to cross the road. My mother, who was driving, was unable to avoid it and it collided with the wing of the car and then ran off down the bank. It was impossible to tell how badly it was injured but we were suddenly surrounded by a group of shouting men wielding sticks and axes. Fortunately this was a Forestry Commission area and we were given shelter in the Forestry Commissioner's house.

After some time, and an impassioned speech in Turkish by my father, a settlement was reached with the sad owner of the cow, who stood cap in hand whilst others argued on his behalf. We never did discover the fate of the cow, but the car had a rather crumpled wing. That day we had lunch consisting almost entirely of beans in a restaurant by a river and spent the night in a rather rudimentary motel. The following day the car suddenly stopped and showed no signs of life. My father left my mother, my sister Susie, and I by the side of the road in a green landscape of willow trees and grazing cows, and hitched a lift to the nearest town an hour away to seek assistance. On his return journey by chance there was a mechanic on board the lorry and he quickly got the car going again and so we reached Ankara. The following day there was a long drive across the Anatolian Plain, through the Gates of Alexander in the Taurus Mountains and down to the coast to Adana to catch our plane to Cyprus.

In Cyprus my parents caught up with several old friends, the Diamantises, Porphyrios Dikaios (now curator of the museum and an expert on Neolithic remains) and the Syrian Mogabgab, who had not wanted to know my father when he was apparently in disgrace but was now all obsequious smiles. For the first time I saw the delights of the land of my birth: classical and medieval sites, ruined marble temples, Bellapais Abbey and the romantic crusader castles of St Hilarion and Buffavento. There were also wildflowers to be enjoyed: asphodels, poppies and multicoloured vetches.

After Cyprus we drove along Turkey's lovely southern shore with deeply wooded slopes on a road that wound in and out of the deeply indented valleys where rivers ran down from the Taurus Mountains to the sea. There were little bays where we could swim and small boys would appear to offer us encrusted ancient coins which they had found on the beach. We bought a few. At night we camped, much to the dismay of the local villagers who told us to beware of evil spirits. We visited various classical sites, and as the handbrake on the car became steadily more unreliable we had to put rocks under the wheels whenever we parked on a slope. After yet another puncture, a garage removed the tyre by running a lorry over it in lieu of a tyre lever.

Susie was very silent throughout this journey. I was shocked when my father told me she had thrown his precious photograph canisters into the sea as we returned from Cyprus. I did not realise that these were early signs of her later full-blown paranoid schizophrenia, although my parents had received a disturbing letter from Bedales (all my siblings followed me there) saying they were worried by her odd behaviour as she had been found walking barefoot in a stream.

After this epic journey I had time in Istanbul to revisit its wealth of classical, Byzantine and Muslim buildings and to buy angora rugs and turquoise plates in the covered market. When it came time to leave, a riot had broken out and the bridges across the Golden Horn had been closed to traffic so we crossed the waterway in a rowing boat with my luggage precariously hanging off the back. We arrived at the station just in time to see the train sliding out. Fortunately the Embassy jeep was there and we set off in pursuit. The train line from Edirne to Istanbul had been built for the Ottoman Empire by Germany before the First World War and the engineers had been paid by the mile, so the line meanders in great loops across the flat marshy plain of European Turkey; it was therefore not difficult to catch up, and I soon boarded.

The journey was without incident until we reached Munich, which I had been looking forward to as my father had promised me a sleeping berth thereafter. Unfortunately I didn't realise that the train had divided into two halves and that my half was terminating there! I struggled round through crowds and boarded-up platforms and put my suitcase on the train and went back for my bundle of rugs and other souvenirs but the train had gone before I could get back. I had managed to miss the same train twice, and was reduced to tears of exhaustion and fright. I had no German but was looked after by a sympathetic woman booking clerk who found me a seat on a later train to Ostend. This was a great relief, except that I had to share my compartment with an excessively lascivious English couple who embarrassed the only other occupant of the carriage so much that she left. I was too tired to protest.

12

PROMOTION

I was always eager for promotion – an attitude that upset some of my fellow constables as they felt it meant that I despised the rank of constable. In fact it was much more complicated than that, as I knew that I was not nearly as good as some of them whose resolve, decency and understanding of human nature often far surpassed my own. I was frequently surprised by the compassion and generosity of my fellow officers towards human failings when I only felt irritation. However, in contrast to my old friends from school I still felt that I was a failure and needed to compensate by being ambitious.

In those days of inadequate schooling, police officers without O Levels had to pass Civil Service exams – Grade 2 for sergeants and Grade 1 for inspectors – before being allowed to take the police promotion exams. Rather to my surprise I found myself giving arithmetic lessons to some of my fellow women constables. For male constables and sergeants the police exams for uniform sergeant and inspector could be taken as competitors, with the top 100 or so being automatically promoted. Those of us in specialist branches (not only women but also CID, traffic and mounted officers) could only qualify and then had to pass a selection board for the limited number of vacancies. Moreover, to become a sergeant one had to have a minimum of five years' service (Graduate Entry and accelerated promotion schemes have now considerably reduced this qualifying time). The police service is one of the few professions where everyone starts at the bottom – very democratic and important for understanding how it feels to be alone on the streets with the great British public in all its varieties.

The Home Office, misguidedly, has constantly tried to introduce direct entry to officer rank by drawing a class-conscious analogy with the armed forces. Under the present class-ridden government, with its excessive admiration for the business world and denigration of public services, they have, alas, minimally succeeded and allowed direct entry of 'experts' to the rank of inspector. They have also used an inappropriate American model to impose expensive Police and Crime Commissioners, elected by a tiny minority, on chief constables in pursuit of greater 'democracy'.

The promotion exams consisted of two parts – the first was effectively a memory test requiring us to reproduce verbatim four or five short passages from the Instruction Book. In preparation we had to learn more than a hundred such potential extracts. The second part, concerning 'knowledge and reasoning', was more fun and posed complex scenarios which we had to resolve citing appropriate law and procedures.

When I had successfully passed both the exam and the selection board, I had only four years' service under my belt. As a result, in the summer of 1961 I was sent as an acting sergeant to Kennington to await my full promotion when my five-year anniversary fell in November. I have little recollection of my first selection board except that one (male) board member asked me exactly the same question twice (it was a warm summer's day) and I tried to give some elegant variation to my response.

My parents returned from Turkey that summer and I spent some time trying to find temporary rented accommodation for them. Initially they were in a flat in Rutland Gate near Hyde Park, where the full horror of my sister Susie's schizophrenia first became apparent – she would not eat for fear of being poisoned and would not come out of her room. Any odd behaviour that she had displayed before that I had put down to adolescence. She ran away from Rutland Gate to Hampshire near Bedales, where she was found wandering, and my father and I went to collect her from a doctor's house in Liphook. Both of us were dreading the encounter, and the doctor did not help my distress by saying she might commit suicide at any time. This was the first of many such flights which ended with her in a mental hospital.

I went house-hunting with my father and we looked at a delightful house among the Nash terraces in Regent's Park (where my mother had been born) but it only had a five-year lease. My parents eventually bought a long lease on an elegant house in Victoria Square just behind Buckingham Palace Mews, so we had the pleasure of military bands marching past most mornings.

There was never any doubt that I would leave the safe anonymity of my room (a bed, table, chair and wash basin) in the Police Section House in Hackney and return to live at home. In the Section House, we had communal bathrooms and some rudimentary cooking facilities – a kettle and a hotplate. (There was a rather poor canteen which I rarely used.) I usually snacked on tomato soup and grated cheese and the occasional delicious stew prepared by my colleague Megan in her terrifying hissing pressure cooker.

I found home life pretty miserable – dominated by Susie's illness and visits to many of London's mental hospitals, where I was often sent in place of my parents. She was initially in St Thomas' Hospital and treated by Dr William Sargant (a well-known expert on brainwashing), who subjected her to the horrors of electro-convulsive therapy, which destroyed her memory. When my mother visited, she was pleased to see Susie smile for the first time for ages but confused by the strange and disturbing questions she asked, such as 'Does the zip in my skirt mean something?' That summer I went to stay with my old school friend Bridget at her parents' house in Kent and burst into tears when I tried to tell her about Susie. I was also terrified that madness might be genetic and that I might go mad too.

Those first three months at Kennington Police Station were tranquil, and I had my first taste of power in being able to grant or refuse requests for 'time off' from my fellow constables! I was then offered a choice of postings as a fully fledged sergeant to either West End Central or to East Ham to cover the whole of K Division, comprising West Ham and East Ham (now Newham), Barking, Romford and Dagenham. I chose the latter without much thought because I wanted to escape from the unhappy young girls and prostitutes I knew from my time in Stepney and on evening shifts at Bow Street.

I had also had a very happy month's attachment to the CID with Winnie (Detective Sergeant) Harrison at East Ham, which, while enjoyable, persuaded me that I wanted neither the hours nor the paperwork entailed in being a CID officer. I was also deterred by the petty but institutional corruption – detectives often invented imaginary informants so that they could pocket the payments due to them and also claimed expenses for long hours of overtime that they had not worked. These claims were approved by their detective inspectors as an acceptable addition to their salaries despite the fact that they also received a Detective Duty Allowance to cover the cost of wearing plainclothes. The CID were very much a separate entity in those days and many changes have since been made to bring them under the control of the generally more disciplined and less corrupt uniform service.

Winnie was a great character who on retirement became a stalwart of the Women's Royal Voluntary Service (now the RVS). On one occasion when we were passing through the charge room there was, mysteriously, a large white bath on the floor. Winnie leapt into it and, seizing a broom from a passing cleaner, began scrubbing her back and singing 'I'm Forever Blowing Bubbles' (West Ham's tribal anthem). She also amused me (and others) by writing entries in the CID's day book such as 'Patrolling the High Street in search of U.F.O.'s'. I was unused to such frivolity in my fellow officers. Winnie was, however, a brilliant and hard-working detective who made many arrests. On one occasion she cooked for me and my parents – my one and only experience of eating tripe and onions.

On my arrival at K Division as a sergeant in 1961 there was no woman inspector, so my fellow woman sergeant and I were jointly responsible for the work and welfare of the women officers on the division. There were two women at each of the six police stations, except at East Ham itself where we had some probationers. Otherwise they were all long-serving women with considerably more service and experience than I. In consequence, I had plenty of time to study for the inspector's exam and to learn to decipher the *Guardian* crossword in my lunch hour. I regularly had lunch with Sergeant Alan Burgess, an amiable bearded giant of a man whose only fault seemed to be a liking for unsuccessful betting on the horses. Long after I left the division he was convicted of shooting dead his wife and mother-in-law.

One of the perks of being on an outer division was that I had to be able to drive a police car. Despite being able to drive already, in the summer of 1962 I was sent on the five-week standard car course at Hendon with a group of other, mostly CID, non-traffic specialist officers. We had a lovely time drawing pretty cross-sections of carburettors for the first three days and having the workings of an internal combustion engine explained to us. There were strings of mnemonics of which I can only remember the start of one: 'When Old Fogey Tries With Fire Extinguisher...' referring to the obligatory checks before taking out a police car – Wheels, Oil, Fuel, Tyres, Water, Fire Extinguisher. Regrettably, I never followed this instruction and blithely assumed that the police car I was taking out was in good shape. At lunchtime we played bowls. Then we had long drives out into the summer countryside with our instructor (there were three novices in each car) telling us not to be so insipid and encouraging me to be a 'ton-up' girl and drive at a hundred miles an hour. I declined. We also had spells on the skid pan, a night drive, and were taught the useful skills of defensive driving.

I remember few exciting incidents from my time on K Division, which then encompassed long streets of terraced houses named after events in the Boer War like Ladysmith and Mafeking.

In the east of the division there were the vast sprawling streets of the Dagenham Estate (when built in the 1930s it was the largest housing estate in the world). Although a laudable attempt to cope with slum clearance from the East End of London and to provide a good standard of housing, it had no provision for pubs, shops or places of entertainment and there was little community spirit. Most people worked for Ford Motors and saw little prospect of escape from an unsympathetic environment. Offences consisted mainly of minor assaults and property crime, along with sexual offences such as indecent exposure.

In those perhaps more innocent times, there did not seem to be organised sexual abuse of children. In some large families we suspected that there were incestuous relationships, with a wife complicit in a father's relationships with his daughters, but since there were no explicit complaints there was little we could do. I do remember one very young girl who approached old men in the park and dismayingly offered herself in exchange for money or sweets. She was taken into care and no one was prosecuted. I was horrified by one family where the wife had seven children which she had difficulty in controlling. She was deeply depressed and urgently needed surgery for a prolapsed womb but her husband would not allow her to have the necessary hysterectomy because it 'would interfere with his matrimonial rights' even though the surgeon advised that having another child might kill her. I had no idea that men then had such rights over their wives' bodies.

The main excitement on the division was the policing of West Ham's football ground, which in those days was wholly performed by male officers. It was the years of their great success when Bobby Charlton was the captain of England and they won the European Cup Winners' Cup, so I was caught up in the universal euphoria and have retained a soft spot for the team ever since. As a superintendent/chief superintendent at Chiswick many years later I spent three years being responsible for the policing of Brentford Football Club and spent many hours with freezing feet standing on their terraces. When I first arrived at Chiswick the chief inspector had a very gung-ho approach to policing at Brentford, where the crowds rarely exceeded 6,000 (although there was some fiddling of crowd numbers as a tax avoidance scheme). The ground was unusual as there were gates at each corner so that fans could move at will between all four sides of the ground and if trouble broke out the 'hooligans' could run all round the ground with the chief inspector and his posse in hot pursuit! I put a stop to that by posting an officer at each of the four corners to intercept anyone wanting to move between the stands. I found that women officers were much better than the men in this position as they were willing to listen and give explanations. Male officers were inclined to say, 'You can't come through because I say so', which only led to further trouble. It was difficult to change the attitudes of men who liked to be authoritative.

There was one exciting event whilst I was at East Ham – a Beatles concert. It was early in their career and I knew nothing about them, unlike the hordes of screaming girls who packed the auditorium. I had a small encounter with a reporter who wanted to know what time they would arrive because it was 'in the public interest'. It was the first time that I distinguished clearly between what interested the public and what might be in the public interest.

The one project on K Division which was of interest whilst I was a sergeant there was the Juvenile Liaison Team stationed at Plaistow. This was an idea that had originated in Liverpool and was intended to divert youngsters from a life of crime. Instead of being taken to court young offenders were, with the agreement of the victim, given a caution and then supervised by one of the three officers (a male sergeant and two constables, a man and a woman) in the team who worked with them and their families. The project was on an experimental basis and was discontinued after I left because it was vigorously opposed by the juvenile court magistrates. Over the years of my service many such preventative schemes have been introduced as part of Neighbourhood or Community Policing Schemes or as part of the duties of Home Beat officers (now called Community Constables). The current Restorative Justice Scheme (first trialled in Milton Keynes) is part of this long tradition of police attempts to prevent crime as first enjoined upon the Metropolitan Police in 1829. When I was the chief superintendent at Chiswick in the early 1980s I gave one of my best Home Beat officers, PC Smooker, two keen young probationers to help him on his difficult beat which had notorious tower blocks with basement garages and a problem of harassment of Asian shopkeepers. Both the incidents of thefts from cars and the harassment by juveniles were almost entirely eliminated.

After two years on K Division, I took and passed the inspector's promotion exam and selection board and was sent on the six-month inspector course at the National Police College at Bramshill. I also began evening classes at Toynbee Hall for the diploma in Criminology that was specifically designed for police and prison officers. Our first year was on criminal law, which we were taught by a kind and earnest barrister named John Freeman. He was disconcerted to find that we knew more about the subject than he did, but he also introduced us to the complexities and perversities of case law as opposed to statute law. I was troubled to discover the poor promotion prospects of the prison officers, who might have to wait fifteen years for promotion to governor level and who hoped that an academic qualification would assist. Their established system of direct graduate entry to governor level meant that, unlike police officers, they had few prospects of promotion.

The second year of our criminology course, on penology, was taught by Louis Blom Cooper and was great fun and full of vigorous arguments. Largely due to him and his book *A Calendar of Murder* I became a member of the Howard League for Penal Reform and a supporter of its campaign against capital punishment; I was later on its council. The cases of Timothy Evans, Christopher Craig and Derek Bentley were of course also influential. Many years later, when I was in the Lords, I had the great pleasure of being with Louis as a guest of the much loved and missed Baroness Serota (the mother of the then Director of the Tate Gallery, Nick Serota) in her lovely house and garden in Hampstead. Louis was as rambunctious as ever. It was on an evening at Toynbee Hall, as I was on my way down the stairs leaving the criminology class, that there was a shout of 'President Kennedy has been assassinated'. As everyone says, you always remember where you first heard that news.

Whilst on K Division I had my first experiences of public speaking, which were usually disastrous! The very first occasion was to a British Legion group, to whom I was supposed to be relating the history of the Metropolitan Women Police. To my surprise, the meeting started with prayers. I had copious notes but gabbled though them in fifteen minutes and then gazed speechlessly at the small audience. Fortunately I somewhat redeemed myself by being more relaxed and anecdotal in answer to questions, but I have never forgotten my initial embarrassment. With practice I did gradually improve, although I do remember one other embarrassing occasion when I had eaten kipper for supper and had a whiskery bone stuck in my throat and so could scarcely speak. It did not help that we were in a vaulted crypt with columns that reflected my enfeebled voice back to me.

In 1962, I was elected as the women sergeants' representative to the Police Federation. This provided companionship and a much wider view of the police service. We were very fortunate in the Met because our chairman, Dick Pamplin, and the treasurer, Peter Joiner, also held those positions in the national organisation. Our domestic discussions seemed always to be about policemen's shirts – whether they should be cotton or nylon, have pockets and long sleeves, and the difficulties that their wives had in washing and ironing them. The five-day National Conference was rather different and dealt with wider issues such as national pay and promotion. My first National Conference, at Easter 1962, was in Blackpool, which was then a flourishing holiday resort. We, the Met delegation, stayed in a traditional boarding house which served excellent food. Tea (a hearty meal) was at six o'clock and a supper of sandwiches was offered last thing in the evening. On the streets there were excellent fish-and-chips shops, and we explored the pier, went up the Tower to see the aquarium and were treated to an evening of entertainment in the Tower Ballroom. At subsequent conferences in Blackpool I have sadly seen it become progressively shabbier and less distinctively northern.

At later conferences in Scarborough in 1963 and Brighton in 1964 I became part of a small gang with three male sergeants.

In Scarborough one of them had a car and we absconded for an afternoon to visit Rievaulx Abbey and to play dominoes in a pub afterwards. I greatly enjoyed their undemanding comradeship. In Brighton, after an evening in a pub, we went paddling in the sea on the stony beach.

At this time I also twice acted as part of the support team for the women going to the Nijmegen marches in Holland in early summer, where teams walk 100 miles in four days (the men do 120). I very much enjoyed the first occasion on the back of a scooter carrying food, water and first-aid supplies. I loved the wildflowers by the roadside and threaded cornflowers, poppies and rest harrow into the brim of my straw hat. The second year was less enjoyable as I was driving an unfamiliar Volkswagen and had to weave my way amongst the hundreds of walkers and cyclists. Moreover I was accompanied by the unresponsive parents of one of the women in our team and they were only interested in her progress and were incompetent map readers.

Life at home was not happy as my parents tried to cope with Susie's schizophrenia, her regular flights from home and further stays in various mental hospitals including that strange Victorian building at Virginia Waters whose mock-Gothic hall has pillars decorated with writhing creepers inhabited by little devils. On one occasion my parents had booked a week's holiday in Ireland and Susie was to go with them, but at the last moment she refused to go. After my parents left I burst into tears.

My father could not bear to be too involved and coped by setting up a trust fund for Susie, of which I remain a trustee, whilst my mother was and remained totally consumed by Susie's illness. Dinah, wisely, was sharing a flat with friends in South Kensington. Tom was having a difficult adolescence and resented the total concentration on Susie. I seized every opportunity to escape, often to France to stay with the Douadys, either at their house at Cavalaire-sur-Mer on the Cote d'Azur or delightfully at Clement-Noel's wedding in Corrèze one December. Since I had several uncles and aunts and more than twenty first cousins there were other avenues for escape and my mother always kept in close touch with her mother, aunts and sisters, which alleviated some of the strain upon her.

13

INSPECTOR

I took and passed the promotion exam and selection board for inspector at the earliest opportunity and began to feel less of a failure (I probably still had my fair share of snobbery about 'other ranks'). I was promoted to inspector in 1965 and was posted back to Central London from what had sometimes felt like exile in the outer suburbs. Caledonian Road was on N Division in Islington borough (in yet another reorganisation of the Met – each new commissioner tampered with the structure – police divisions had now been aligned with the London boroughs).

Before that I had attended the six-month inspector course at the National Police College at Bramshill in Hampshire, which was a wonderful and liberating experience for me as I had been too tightly focussed on police work and longed to be part of a wider community of artists and intellectuals as I imagined my parents had been, but I could see no way of entering that vanished world.

My police career was to be further punctuated by time at Bramshill – with two years as a member of the teaching staff and on further courses. Bramshill House was in the main (there were medieval foundations) an early seventeenth-century mansion built by Edward de la Zouche, allegedly for the then Prince of Wales, Henry, the eldest son of James I. The statue of the founder is on the back of the mansion gazing over the rose garden (de la Zouche was a keen botanist) and Prince of Wales feathers can be seen in the stonework over the front door. I came to love the mansion and when I was on the staff had the great pleasure of showing visitors around and pointing out the Brussels tapestries, the strap work ceilings and the curious feathered decoration in the long gallery. The mansion also had a deer park with white fallow deer and, from time to time, peacocks (which usually escaped) on the terrace. This splendid mansion was government property and has of course since been sold.

The classrooms and student accommodation were in modern buildings scattered along the side of the lake, which was said to be inhabited by large pike that ate the baby ducklings and, more agreeably, the goslings of the flocks of Canada geese whose droppings fouled the short turf around the lake.

The course for eighty prospective inspectors from all over the country was divided into two, with the first three months a liberal arts course with lessons on history, politics and the social sciences. At that stage in the early sixties very few police officers were graduates and many had left school at fifteen, so the intention was to give a wider perspective to future police leaders. Indeed, we mostly had talks from retired military men on that nebulous quality, leadership, which usually consisted of a suggested long list of qualities (courage, a sense of humour, integrity, and so on) which just made me and others feel inadequate as no one could possess all those qualities. By the time that I came back on the staff in 1973 there was a greater acceptance that different styles of leadership could be effective. Some speakers were truly inspirational, such as Viscount Slim, whose clarity and compassion meant that I would happily have followed him into the jungles of Burma where he had made his reputation.

One of the most unforgettable lessons, always referred to when reminiscing by those who witnessed the performance, was the history lecture called 'The River of Time'. All the way down the centre of the Assembly Hall was a long blue cloth with salient events, dynasties, battles and dates arranged along it from the ancient Egyptians to the present day, and two members of staff who had been majors in the Army Education Corps ran up and down recounting dramatic events in the history of the Western World (Asia and Africa did not feature very much). It gave a splendidly memorable but traditional and Eurocentric view of human history. I was grateful for this lesson, which organised my very scattered knowledge, but I felt out of step with other officers who were impatient about what they saw as 'airy-fairy' nonsense and wanted to get back to the practical reality of police subjects. When I defended the recently introduced system of comprehensive schools, the Special Branch sergeant sitting next to me said I must be a Communist and asked what I was doing in the police service. I silently wondered how someone with such rigid views could be in Special Branch.

The second half of the course was, more mundanely, devoted to police topics such as public order policing, traffic and criminal investigation including a lecture from a pathologist whose main aim seemed to be to shock us with accounts of maggots and decomposition. It was the early days of the introduction of breathalysers and some of the men were asked to drink several pints of beer to demonstrate how they functioned. On one large detective sergeant it had no apparent affect at all, which puzzled the investigators.

When I arrived at the age of twenty-nine as an inspector at Caledonian Road Police Station on N Division in 1965, I had two women sergeants and about fifteen policewomen stationed at Kings Cross (my old station), Islington and Caledonian Road. The two sergeants were older than me and more experienced so did most of the supervision and training of our young policewomen. The sergeant stationed at Kings Cross was a difficult woman who clearly resented my appointment. She had an embittered outlook on life and I don't think it was just due to my age or other inexperience. My other sergeant was pleasant enough but tended to give long-winded explanations to our young probationers and if interrupted would always start again at the beginning.

I chiefly remember Caledonian Road for its excellent canteen, where we had home-cooked lunches unlike the watery peas and fry-ups of earlier canteens, and how we had horses stationed there – always so useful when coping with a lost child. I remember one horrendous case of a woman who had killed her six-year-old daughter by fracturing her skull. The detective inspector told me that the girl was half-starved since all the mother's attention had been lavished on her eight-year-old son. The girl had twice been to hospital with injuries which had not been reported to police or social services. The hospital had merely sent a hospital almoner round who had not been allowed into the house. Such a case would today occasion an outcry about the incompetence of the authorities but it attracted very little attention and the mother pleaded guilty and was sentenced to a long term in prison.

Whilst on N Division I was distracted and diverted by extra-curricular activities. I was invited by the then head of the women police, Chief Superintendent Shirley Beck, to write a semi-autobiographical book about my early career as part of a series intended as vocational guidance for sixth-formers. It was later published in both hardback and paperback as *The Gentle Arm of the Law*. As it had to be vetted by Scotland Yard, it is a necessarily rather anodyne account and I was not allowed to identify any officers by name. Nevertheless it was a fascinating experience and I enjoyed the discussions with the agent and publisher, although I was criticised – as more recently – for not making it emotional enough!

I also embarked on the third year of my criminology diploma on the psychology of crime, which I found fascinating. I became friendly with our teacher, Joyce Prince, and her family and had several enjoyable and argumentative dinner parties at her house. I continued to be a women's federation representative but found the inspectors' conferences more formal and I no longer had my little band of convivial fellow sergeants. It was, however, a time of great upheaval in the police service of England and Wales – more than a hundred forces (including many small borough forces) were being reduced to the forty-three we have today. The Home Office was also introducing an Accelerated Promotion Scheme and a special course at Bramshill for bright young sergeants. This was bitterly resented by the inspectors at the conference, who insisted that everyone should spend as long as they had (in one case fifteen years!) as a sergeant before promotion to inspector.

During my second year as an inspector, Bramshill Police College invited applications to be an instructor on the staff. I was interviewed by a daunting array of about a dozen chief constables chaired by the then president of the Association of Chief Police Officers, Sir Edward Dodd (a lovely man who sadly died young of an asthma attack). I did not have high hopes of being successful so was not very anxious about the outcome and therefore perhaps came across as confident. Sir Edward asked me what I thought I could contribute to the staff and I rather tentatively said that I sometimes had radical ideas contrary to the usual run of police thinking. He turned to Robert Mark (later to be a reforming Commissioner of the Metropolitan Police) and said, 'That sounds like you, Bob.' To my surprise, they all laughed. I think it was the laughter that encouraged them to accept me.

There was then a four-week instructor's course with a rather sketchy outline of teaching methods. The year before, the police service had given university scholarships to two young officers (one of whom, Geoff Dear, went on to be the Chief Constable of the West Midlands and later on joined me in the House of Lords). In its second year, more Bramshill Scholarships were to be awarded. My fortuitous presence on the instructor's course reminded the Police College that I existed, and I was offered a scholarship. Most scholarships were for degrees in law or economics, but I was keen to study psychology, partly because of Susie's illness. Eventually a place was found for me at Manchester University.

14

MANCHESTER UNIVERSITY

In September 1967, I arrived at Manchester University and moved into lodgings. It was the time of radical student movements throughout Europe and of protests about the Vietnam War, so I expected my fellow students to be argumentative left-wing activists, but I was disappointed – they were mostly apolitical and rather shy.

As well as my main course in psychology we were required to do three subsidiary subjects. I plumped for French and philosophy, where I thought I would have a head start, and history of art, where at last I could follow my own interests. Our first lesson with Professor Dodgson, an expert on the art of the Middle Ages, was terrifying as he said we needed to be fluent in Latin, French and German before we could hope to be art historians! Fortunately this was mainly directed at those among us who were doing the subject as their main degree. I continued this subsidiary into my second year and went on to do a diploma in the history of art on my return to London.

I enjoyed my psychology course, and though distracted at the same time by two brief love affairs with women who were not interested in politics, travel or the arts, I acquired a respectable 2:1 degree. I particularly enjoyed the comparative studies of animal behaviour and the accounts of Tinbergen and Lorenz – goslings who fell in love with yellow wellington boots – and the 'superstitious' goose who always stopped halfway up some stairs as though it had seen a ghost. The behaviour of three-spined sticklebacks also came in useful when I was on the staff at the Police College and taught a series of lessons on developmental psychology.

The head of the psychology department, Professor John Cohen, was an expert on cognitive psychology – his book *Chance, Skill and Luck* was required reading with its accounts of the behaviour of professional footballers and bus drivers. He had also done some fascinating experiments on time perception with an explanation for the regularly observed phenomenon that journeys to a destination always seem to take longer than the return trip. There was also an obligatory course in applied statistics which some of my fellow students found difficult. I had more problems with the studies on crowd behaviour and group psychology (which should have had considerable relevance for a police officer), finding the conclusions shallow and uninspiring. Studying crowd behaviour in a controlled laboratory setting is of course impossible, so the research largely depended on personal anecdotes from participants. There was the interesting suggestion that being in a crowd heightens adrenaline flows and increases excitement and contagious behaviour, which can lead to abrupt changes of mood, but I already knew that the policy of police should always be to stay calm and if possible avoid confrontation. The accounts of Milburn's experiments, which showed the extent to which people are willing to inflict suffering if ordered by a person apparently in authority (wearing a lab coat, for example) I found particularly disturbing, with its implications for a uniformed service.

Manchester, that great northern city, felt like a foreign country. There were still mill chimneys in some of the dales and row upon row of terraced houses throughout the city. There were also vacant bomb sites onto which the university has since expanded. The vibrant cultural traditions of the city were all around in the Whitworth and City Art Galleries and the medieval Rylands Library. I went to performances of *Peer Gynt* and saw Laurence Olivier playing Shylock but, curiously, have no memory of going to the cinema in all the four years I was in Manchester, although I did join the university film club and saw some foreign films like Bergman's *Wild Strawberries* and Jacques Tati's immortal comedies. When I felt lonely I used to go to the top of the university museum, where there was a small aquarium, and commune silently with the fish and a small blue-spotted gecko which viewed me suspiciously though its slit eyes.

In my third year my social life improved. There were now six other police officers on Bramshill Scholarships, variously studying sociology, economics and law, and we met for lunch in the student refectory every Thursday, where I regularly had cheese salad and chips. We were often now joined by Sonja Hunt, who had returned to Manchester for postgraduate study, and who considerably enlivened our meal with her radical anti-establishment and anti-police views. She became a lifelong friend. It was probably about this time that I wrote a poem about the pleasures of lively conversation

A good
Conversation
Divides a topic

Like a filleted herring
The backbone
The main line of discussion
The rib bones
Neatly terminated side issues
The fish-flesh of emotion
The stew of unreason
Make conversation
A bouillabaisse.

I had become friends with Sonja and her gentle husband, Joe, when she returned to the university in my third year to do a master's. She was studying hypnosis, and gave a demonstration to my class which showed the power of suggestibility. I was one of her victims, and while I was 'under' she told me to imagine sucking a lemon, which predictably made my mouth go dry. With Sonja and Joe, I began to explore the rolling hills of the Peak District and lovely Dovedale. We also regularly visited countryside pubs, such as the Frozen Mop, and as Joe drove us home Sonja and I sang out of tune in the back of the car. Joe was a great craftsman and made himself a beautiful guitar in inlaid wood. I was sad when some years later I heard that he had died. Sonja moved to live in the United States and I had memorable holidays with her in Arizona and Pennsylvania.

For some of the police officers, university was a totally life-changing affair. I felt less of an academic failure and gained confidence in my ability to learn new facts. Some, like Dave Phillips, embraced it with great flair and enthusiasm, but others found it more traumatic. I particularly remember Bill, a rather stiff and conventional Manchester officer who stayed at home with his family, who said that his whole attitude to bringing up his children had been changed and that he was now more tolerant and flexible. I became a student representative and so attended staff meetings of the psychology department. This experience totally disillusioned me about the supposed cloistered calm of academe. The staff bickered and squabbled and made rambling and inconsequential arguments.

Some police officers as a result of their time at university left the police service and became lecturers. However, quite apart from my profound sense of obligation to the police service, I also realised that I would miss the decisiveness and challenge of dealing with policing problems. This feeling was reinforced by my research year, which I found peculiarly solitary and unchallenging as I had no one with whom I could discuss my findings.

Rather oddly, and inexplicably, the police service gave me, unlike any other officer before or since, a fourth year at Manchester to do research (other officers subsequently tried to use this as a precedent but without success). Professor Cohen wrote to the then Commissioner of the Met, Sir John Waldron, who was given to making unconsidered decisions, allegedly in his bath. The surprising positive response was that I should do research in either the race relations or juvenile fields. I chose to combine the two and to look at the employment hopes of black and ethnic minority school-leavers. The received wisdom at the time was that 'immigrants' had unrealistic ambitions and that this accounted for their feelings of resentment and disappointment.

I showed fairly conclusively (and later wrote an article for the magazine *Race Today*) that both white and black boys were equally unrealistic. They all wanted apprenticeships in various branches of engineering and there were only three apprenticeships on offer in Manchester that year. One white boy, more realistically, wanted to be a baker. The only group in my study who had dreams beyond the likelihood of fulfilment were the Asian girls, all of whom wanted to be doctors to increase their bride-price. Since my research was in a secondary modern school with no sixth form, and where the pupils rarely achieved even O Levels, this was tragically unlikely.

During that year, 1971, Sonja and I were asked to teach psychology to a group of nurses who were embarking on a degree (recently introduced) in nursing, as they had been abandoned by their teacher halfway through the academic year. I particularly remember a lesson I attempted to give on stereotypes and why generally society is more amused by the deaf than the blind but was soundly berated by one of the students who said it was not amusing to be deaf. In vain I tried to explain but was shouted down. Sonja and I tried to find a suitable textbook that would be both comprehensive and pitched at a suitable level for the non-specialist; two years later, when I was on the staff at the Police College, this led to us jointly writing a psychology textbook called *Individual Development and Social Experience*. Sonja would send me reams of undigested scientific material for each chapter and I would attempt to render it in more comprehensible language. The subsequent book was sufficiently successful to run to a second edition and a paperback.

Sonja later moved to various teaching and research posts in both Britain and the United States but has remained an amusing and entertaining friend with a refreshingly anarchic view of the world. Most of her research has been on the overlap between medicine and society – looking at the effect of poor housing on children's health, for example. She is currently in her eighties and learning Arabic, German and Hebrew. Before she went to America we spent a week's holiday together in Pembrokeshire in 1972 and I wrote a poem about Sonja's reluctance to categorise nature – it should, she said, just be 'experienced' – I find echoes of this idea in the current craze for 'mindfulness' (and of course in Blake's and Keats' view that Newton had destroyed the romance of the rainbow).

In balance between sea and air
The rock-hard cliffs and
Black shattered slates hold me.
A cold North wind over the sea
Buffets me sideways again –
I am entirely alive and aware
That the delicate bones of my skull
Would crunch on that rock beneath
Crushing my sensible, senseless brain.

I crawl clumsily over the top
Gorse spiking my knee
The coconut smell of the flowers
Hot in the calm of the lee.
Sonja lies dreaming again
Whilst I catalogue what I see-
Violets and vetch, thrift, a black beetle,
And delight – a lizard feels free
With black, unblinking stare
To catalogue me.

15

RETURN TO THE MET

After my four years at university, I returned to London in the autumn of 1971 and bought a semi-detached Edwardian house in Teddington. My father had by now retired and my parents had moved out to Wiltshire on the hill above the National Trust village of Lacock, with a view to the distant hills around Bath. Theirs was a rather isolated house lying between two farms and I think my father found this more depressing than my mother, who was a great user of the telephone to keep in touch with her sisters and their families. I, like my father, was not good at keeping up a long telephone conversation. My father found some solace in becoming president of the National Schizophrenia Society and from his membership of the Aristotelian Society, for whom he wrote a published article called 'Indeterminate Determinacy' (which I found incomprehensible).

Coming back to a disciplined organisation after four carefree years at university was mildly depressing. Moreover, now that my parents were living out of London I was largely responsible for Susie and for coping with the regular crises that occurred when she stopped taking her pills. She was living in a studio flat in Islington near two lots of our cousins who lived in houses in Canonbury, which in the early seventies was already a smart place to live.

I still live in the house in Teddington, and although it now has a second bathroom and a rather larger sitting room it still retains some agreeable Edwardian features like plaster mouldings and stained glass in the front door. It also has a garden with a large pond. The retired Royal Engineer who lived here with his wife had a passion for concrete, and the garden was covered with concrete paths (my brother and a cousin broke them up with pickaxes but I still find little bits of concrete in the flower beds) and a 'swimming pool' – all of 14 feet long – which I rapidly converted into a fish pond.

When I was house-hunting there was a great shortage of houses for sale and potential buyers were being gazumped with offers above the asking price. This did not happen to me but I did not dare attempt to bargain down the price of £9,500 (now notionally worth one million) and to save time I did not have the house surveyed, which was a serious error. It rapidly became apparent that the breakfast room and kitchen were riddled with dry-rot – a large rose-red fungus bloomed behind a curtain and white foam seethed out of the woodwork and the floorboards wept into the cavity below. It was now clear why the skirting boards had been covered over with a secondary layer. The problem was cured with additional ventilation and eventually a solid concrete floor in the kitchen, but I had nightmares for some time about the whole house being swallowed in weeping white foam.

Since I could not move in immediately I had a difficult six weeks of lodging briefly with each of my sisters, which was not easy – especially with Susie, who eyed me suspiciously – and for a week camping at Crystal Palace from where I made my way to my initial posting at Cannon Row Police Station. Fortunately, I had not yet been issued with a new uniform, so I could creep out of my tent in anonymous plainclothes. Two days before I was due to move into my new house, the engineer's wife had a stroke and died within twenty-four hours, but despite this tragedy the sale went ahead. This might have seemed an ill omen, but in fact I have been happy living here and have become a keen gardener.

The Met was not sure what to do with me but after a few weeks at Cannon Row – behind the old Scotland Yard buildings on the Embankment, now an extension of Parliament's buildings – I was posted to Hammersmith in January 1972. This was a traumatic time for many policewomen. The Equal Pay and Equal Opportunities Acts meant that policewomen were now paid the same as policemen and were expected to perform the same hours and duties and no longer to be considered as specialists dealing mainly with women and children. Local Authorities were now employing social workers to deal with children and families in their community, so much of the preventative work that policewomen had previously carried out was swept aside. I sympathised but did not find the transition from a specialist role difficult as I had always disliked being confined to a female role and my early experience in Stepney had been in general duties and street patrol.

However, there were problems of morale for many policewomen as they felt that their previous role had been devalued and insufficiently understood. Some individuals particularly suffered – one of my women sergeants at Hammersmith with nearly thirty years' service was placed in the Traffic Department, which she hated. Soon after, on retirement, she moved to the Isle of

Wight with her husband, who tragically died almost immediately. I felt very sad for her.

Some tasks were much less well performed by the men, who generally saw them as women's work and therefore unimportant. The register of missing persons at each station had been meticulously kept by policewomen who also carried out the relevant enquiries and notified the Central Registry at Scotland Yard. We knew our regular absentees and their families, as running away from home (most were teenagers) was often indicative of more profound problems, and occasionally a 'missing person' turned out to be a murder victim. I found that records were now written up by whichever station officer happened to be on front-counter duties. The entries lacked detail and evinced little sympathy for distressed parents, and it was not at all clear who was responsible for making further enquiries. The other problem was that Hammersmith Council did not have enough social workers to deal with difficult families and their children. The consequence of this was that there was a lack of liaison with other organisations, including the police service. Information was not shared, and this had the potential for the sort of tragedies that have occurred in other London boroughs since.

I enjoyed my extra-curricular activities at Hammersmith. Once a week on Fridays I became the Court Inspector at the Juvenile Court in Marylebone Road and was, for the first time, responsible for the conduct of male officers and their presentation of evidence. Some of them seemed very young and callow. I had come back from university more critical of my fellow officers, and this was the era when corruption scandals were beginning to shake the Met, with stories of manufactured evidence such as that by Sergeant Challoner who had arrested a man and then put half-bricks in his pockets to suggest that he was about to commit a smash-and-grab raid. There were also stories about the overly close relationship between the senior officers running the 'Clubs Office' at West End Central Police Station and the owners of gambling clubs and drinking dens. Notoriously, a masonic lodge had been set up that was peopled entirely by senior detectives and nightclub owners, and it was assumed that they did each other favours. Freemasonry was not as widespread a problem in the Met as in some other police forces, but many years later a commissioner was to decree that membership was incompatible with being a police officer. I was horrified by these newspaper stories but assumed that blatant corruption was isolated to West End Central and the club district.

I also discovered that some of the officers at Hammersmith found it amusing to taunt the homeless men who lived in Butterworth Lodge – the local hostel for down-and-outs. My earlier experience of police aggression was at Leman Street, where there was general respect for the police service. People turned to us for help (which was often provided in the form of a bed for the night or donation of the fare home) but understood that any assault on a police officer would lead to retaliation. A sort of rough justice prevailed, and in the days before personal radios and panda cars individual officers were uniquely vulnerable, so if they were attacked when making an arrest the prisoner could expect to be beaten once in the police station. I was only aware of this happening on one or two occasions during the two years I was at Leman Street.

One consequence of my degrees in psychology was that the police service assumed that I had unique insights into human behaviour. During the obscenity trial of the publishers of the

'Linda Lovelace' book which described prostitution and oral sex, I spent an enjoyable week supposedly advising the prosecuting counsel on the merits or demerits of the defence case. The defence, represented by flamboyant Geoffrey Robinson QC, were claiming that pornography could be therapeutic and cathartic, a theory that was based on some Swedish studies. I did my best to debunk the science involved but was not too surprised when the jury acquitted the publisher, probably on the grounds that the book was only mildly pornographic. Perhaps ironically, many years later, in the 1980s, I would be in charge of the Obscene Publications Branch at New Scotland Yard.

The other rather odd job that I did was 'Snacking' in the Control Room in Scotland Yard for major demonstrations. There had been incidents of bad police behaviour when officers were tired and hungry, notably at one of the major CND rallies in Trafalgar Square when the demonstrators sat down and refused to move and after many hours police officers had become irritable and abusive. A senior appointment from the Army Catering Corps was made, and thereafter all officers were fed a meal before going to a major demonstration and then were given opportunities for snacks and comfort breaks. My job in the control room was to keep track of which groups had been 'snacked' and ensure that no one group went too long without refreshment. The Control Room had banks of video screens so that I had a bird's-eye view of what was happening in Trafalgar Square and in Whitehall. Most protest marches and demonstrations were orderly and controlled by their marshals, but occasionally wild disorder would break out as in the children's demonstration, which had policemen hopelessly pursuing swift teenagers as they ran back and forth across London's bridges. The man in charge was often Jim Starrit, the assistant commissioner, a tall and upright man, who was a noted disciplinarian – on one occasion, when he said he was going home to do some gardening the sergeant in front of me muttered, 'I bet even the onions in his garden come up in straight rows.'

After a year at Hammersmith, I was promoted to chief inspector and took up the post on the staff at Bramshill Police College that I had been selected for before I went to university. The attempt to have Susie living alone had finally broken down, and her neighbours complained about her increasingly strange behaviour. She had forcibly broken a window and when being removed from her flat hit a policeman on the nose. After another stay in hospital she went to live with my parents in Wiltshire, where she was to remain with occasional stays in hospital until their deaths twenty-five years later.

16

POLICE STAFF COLLEGE

Returning to Bramshill at the beginning of 1973 was in some ways a delight as I loved the mansion and its surroundings of parkland and rolling Hampshire countryside, which reminded me to some extent of my life at nearby Bedales. However, I found the culture at the Police Staff College old-fashioned and rigid. It had always been a joke that the college's purpose was to teach police officers to be gentlemen and 'not to eat peas off a knife'!

My fellow members of staff were split into two groups. There were the civilians, responsible for the liberal studies that I had so much enjoyed on my inspectors course and a new department of management studies, and then there was the police department, staffed by officers from various parts of the country, who taught traditional legal and operational courses.

Many of the civilian staff had been army officers in the Second World War and still had very old-fashioned ideas about dress and behaviour. The police students were required to wear dinner jackets for three formal dinners each term, an unnecessary expense which bore hard on the fathers of young families – with some trepidation I joined a small protest group of fellow officers and went to see the commandant, but it was to no avail. I was also furious that at these formal dinners the 'ladies' at the top table were required to withdraw whilst the 'gentlemen' drank their port. This genteel practice was led by the commandant's wife – a beautiful but, I thought, rather silly woman – and was abandoned when we had a new commandant.

The police officers on the staff were in the middle ranks of chief inspector and superintendent from forces outside the Met who saw the time on the staff as a way of enhancing their promotion prospects. This certainly did not apply to Met officers, who once out of sight were out of mind. Whilst on this detachment to the Home Office I ceased to be a police officer, but if I committed a disciplinary offence I would have been instantly returned to the Met. I was told that if I wished to attend a promotion board I would have to leave the Police College.

The commandant was John Alderson, a man of liberal ideas who later became Chief Constable of Devon and Cornwall. The media regularly contrasted him with James Anderton, the Chief Constable of Greater Manchester, who was a disciplinarian of the old school but much admired by his men, on behalf of whom he fought many battles with the Home Office. John Alderson saw me as a natural ally in his desire to promote more egalitarian ideas in the police service and greater opportunities for creative and original thinking. However, he did not seem to understand that some police officers were more comfortable just obeying orders. Much later, when I was a deputy to Richard Wells, DAC (deputy assistant commissioner) in North West London, I found that he had absorbed John Alderson's ideas. He never gave orders, so we had hours of fruitless discussion whilst he tried to persuade us all to his point of view.

The management studies department was run by Mike Plumridge, a nice but rather ineffectual man who was often hurt and confused by the attitudes of many of the police students. They did not like studies of newfangled ideas about management styles and organisations and what they called 'airy-fairy' nonsense. I was part of Mike's team and sympathised with his difficulties but always hoped he would display more robustness in the face of his critics.

At first, the Police College was not sure how to employ me and I had fun running short courses on developmental psychology for the bright young sergeants on the accelerated promotion special course and talking about the courting behaviour of three-spined sticklebacks. My course was also an optional extra for the inspectors. As I was keen on comparative animal studies, I would start with a brief introduction to evolution. To my astonishment, on the first course I found I had three fundamentalists who believed in the Biblical account of Creation. Two of them were Roman Catholics and one woman was an evangelical Christian. I consulted the elderly padre, who said evolution was not accepted by the Catholic Church. However, he went away and consulted higher authority and had the considerable grace to come back and tell me that the facts of evolution were now accepted. I had no such success with the evangelical Christian.

Because of my degrees in psychology, I was regularly given books to review for the college magazine. I therefore learnt an uncomfortable amount about Mary Bell, the killers of Jamie Bulger, and Ian Brady and Myra Hindley. Many years later I was having lunch at the Long Table in the House of Lords, sitting opposite Lord Longford, who had been visiting Myra Hindley in prison. When he said he thought she should be released, I said,

'Certainly not as her crimes are unpardonable.' He replied, 'You lack compassion. I shall pray for you.'

When John Alderson left the college at the end of my first year to take charge in Devon and Cornwall, his successor as commandant established a more traditional regime. Mike Plumridge's department had other police officers with social science degrees attached to it and lessons became more formal.

There was a lack of sensitivity to race relations in the police service at this time. For example, Enoch Powell was invited to address one of the courses. This was justified as an attempt to introduce the students to controversial alternative viewpoints, but too often the invited speakers chimed with prevalent police views. The Brixton riots in 1981 did bring home to the police service that race relations were an important issue, and much more effort has since gone into improving relationships. However, results have been mixed and the Met still has far too few recruits from black and minority ethnic backgrounds.

Other speakers were much more inspiring. Shirley Williams gave a brilliant talk without notes to the Senior Command Course on alternative political groups outside the main contenders for election and really seemed to uncover hidden trends in society (how prescient this now seems!). This was the era of Militant's attempts to infiltrate the Labour Party. In a doomed attempt to challenge police stereotypes and frames of reference, I tried without success to get officers to read magazines such as *Race Today* and *Gay News* but was met with antagonism as my class were determined that there was only one 'right' way to view the world. I felt depressed and discomfited by this experience.

Another attempt was made by Mike Plumridge to break down some of these entrenched attitudes. A management 'guru' called John Heron was hired (probably at great expense) to conduct group sessions with course members. He had a theory that everyone has bubbles of painful thought or feelings trapped within them and that getting these to 'pop out' would create more effective human beings. For police officers reared on concepts of stiff upper lips and self-restraint, his ideas were anathema. I endured several painful sessions in his group meetings where any contribution I might make was rejected with 'You don't understand' or 'You haven't felt enough collars'. Some of the antagonism was possibly due to underlying sexism or hostility to the whole experience. Some of John Heron's rules for group interaction were useful – such as never to claim that everyone agrees by saying 'we think' or 'all right-minded people think' rather than 'I think'. I am still irritated when people assume that I am on their side in an argument, which brings out the worst in my perverse nature! This led to yet another poem:

Why daily must I thus perform
The leaden moves that others ask?
Why resentfully conform
To sober words and serious task
That bind me down and so deform
The self behind the public mask
But what is self and what is mask
That is what I ever ask?

I began to have an increasing dislike of rote exchanges with other members of staff. Too often after a break or weekend away I would be passed in a corridor by someone saying, 'Had a good weekend?' and they would be gone before I could open my mouth to reply.

Naughtily, I began to subvert this practice by giving real answers to these questions. I remember one January (probably 1974) I was standing in the hall waiting for students to arrive when a fellow staff member asked, 'Had a good Christmas?' and instead of saying, 'Lovely, thankyou' I launched into a description of the horrors of my family Christmas with a mentally ill sister, sibling rivalry and my martyr complex as I did all the cooking. It was very unkind. Christmases at home were always fraught with unresolved emotions as we sought for my mother's attention. For most years since then, kind friends have supplied me with presents of jigsaw puzzles, model kits and other distractions to resolve the tensions.

One bright spot in my time on the staff was my developing friendship with Pauline Low, a Bristol and Avon officer who had also had a police scholarship but to study sociology. She came on a course when I was there and succeeded me on the Police College Directing Staff. She first made an impression by saying she wanted to travel to China, and we did indeed twice go to China together.

It is our first holiday to India (and I have been many times since) that is really illuminated in my memory. In addition to the usual triangle of Red Fort, Taj Mahal and Fatipur Sikri, we went to Kashmir with its floating gardens and romantic Mogul Gardens, to Nepal with its extraordinary temples and to Sikkim where we slept in a Buddhist monastery and saw a rosy dawn illuminating the many peaks of Kangchenjunga in succession. Pauline was a delightful travelling companion, always better than I am at striking up conversations (often in sign language) with local people, and we had many more fascinating holidays together. Since then I have had other travelling companions, including our lovely Italian art teacher, Mariella, who has tried in vain to teach me how to paint in watercolours. For some years now I have travelled with the Royal Society for Asian Affairs to Far Eastern countries.

At the end of my two years on the staff, at the beginning of 1975, I returned to the Met and was posted to the Management Services department. With hindsight I should perhaps have requested a different posting as my apparent lack of operational experience later led indirectly to my disastrous year at Battersea.

17

MANAGEMENT SERVICES

This was a fairly new department in the Metropolitan Police Service, detached from the headquarters at New Scotland Yard and accommodated in offices near the Marylebone Road. Our leader was a civilian psychologist, John Lloyd-Jones, a gentle man who was constantly baffled by police culture and organisation. We were a loosely knit group of about fifteen civilians and police officers doing various sorts of research, and I adapted rapidly to its non-hierarchical and convivial nature. Computers were just beginning to be used, although programming seemed to be idiosyncratic and our various 'experts' all had their favourite systems. Some of the research (using car tyres to contain explosions, for example) was ill-directed and duplicated research that had already been done elsewhere or by the Home Office. Our tasks were not eased by the inability of senior police officers to articulate exactly what research they needed.

I was put there to conduct research into recruitment and wastage from the Met. It was a time of high employment so the police service was well below strength and the perennial problem was that we were not attracting enough graduates or candidates from ethnic minorities to fully represent London's population. In my early years in the Met we had a lot of officers from Ireland and Scotland because of high unemployment in those countries, but those sources had dried up. It was therefore important to recruit more officers and retain those we had recruited and trained. Some young recruits were leaving after two or three days at the Training School at Hendon where I was much later to be the commandant.

I was very much left to my own devices by John Lloyd-Jones. By dint of questionnaires and examination of our recruitment procedures and the training school, I was able to make some practical and helpful suggestions. I found, for example, that some of the civilian staff in the recruitment centre were acting as unofficial gatekeepers and weeding out any applicant with a foreign-sounding name. At the Training School at Hendon, the bewildered recruits were subjected to pep talks by as many as fifteen different instructors during their first three days; I recommended that this number should be greatly reduced. Homesickness was also a problem for some of the younger recruits, aged nineteen or twenty, who had never been away from home before. I had some difficulty in explaining my results to the commandant, who had apparently never seen a histogram before and had trouble with percentages.

I was unable to change some practices. The senior officers who sat on recruitment boards often had very fixed ideas about what made an ideal recruit. One chief superintendent said to me that as the candidate came through the door he always tried to imagine him wearing a helmet. This must have disqualified most women candidates. I found equally stereotypical attitudes many years later when I, as a commander, sat on selection boards for the Senior

Command Course and was accompanied by some chief constables who thought they could make instant judgements of a candidate's ability. By then I had the confidence to offer my arguments more forcibly.

I was also part of a working party seeking to introduce a national application form so that potential recruits to different forces could supply the same information about themselves. We made considerable progress towards achieving this objective until I attended a meeting at the Home Office with representatives from other forces and was told at the end of the meeting that the next one would be in twelve months' time! This different sense of urgency was particularly difficult for police officers. On one occasion I gave a talk to social workers in West London and pointed out that some of our difficult relationships with them were due to our different time scales – police officers wanting instant solutions during their tour of duty and social workers taking a much longer-term view of a family with problems or the difficulties of a troubled teenager.

One of the advantages of the regular hours at Management Services was that I was able to go to evening classes again and I embarked on a diploma in the history of art. That first year was on the art of Greece and Rome, and I remember with fondness a particular lesson on the sex lives of monsters! At the end of a happy two years I passed a promotion board and was posted as a superintendent to West Drayton on the Airport Division, where we covered the area around Heathrow.

18

AIRPORT DIVISION

Until two years before 1977, when I was posted there, Heathrow Airport had been policed by the British Airports Police, but due to a variety of factors such as terrorism, the threat of a rocket attack on El Al planes and the need for better coordination with the surrounding areas they had been absorbed into the Metropolitan Police. This was much resented by many of their older officers, but some younger and more ambitious ones saw it as an opportunity to have a more interesting career and were transferred away from the airport. I was posted to West Drayton, which controlled the perimeter area from Feltham in the north to Staines in the south.

This was my first opportunity to experience police management at close quarters and to be in direct operational command of men as well as women. I had expected to have difficulty in managing grizzled male veteran sergeants but found that on the whole rank trumped gender. Moreover, in the police service in demanding situations it is personal qualities that count. To my dismay, my chief difficulties were with my fellow superintendents and chief inspectors, who saw me as a rival for promotion or suggested that my career had been enhanced by sexual favours.

My immediate boss, Ch.Supt Grey, was a relaxed if not rather lazy man at the end of his service who nevertheless had a firm grasp of potential disasters and was very supportive of our fellow officers. For example, when a burglar who was being chased by police jumped into a basement area and broke a leg, he contrived a report that considerably diminished the role of the pursuing officers. This attitude of course has the attendant dangers of cover-ups, opaqueness, and an assumption that the police can do no wrong. I was often surprised that with his maturity and nearly thirty years' service he remained subservient to a senior officer. Often at about six o'clock, when he was just preparing to go home, the commander of the division at Heathrow would summon him to an 'urgent' conference – which was of course just a drinking session.

Some things at the station had become very casual. I was horrified one day when 'checking the books' (seeing what actions and records had been created the previous day) to open a drawer in the station officer's desk and find it contained two loaded firearms. Because of the threat to El Al flights from terrorists allegedly armed with SAM missiles, the outer perimeter of the airport was always patrolled by armed officers whenever an El Al flight was taking off or landing. They had fallen into the habit of handing over their weapons to the next patrol by leaving them in the desk drawer. Subsequently, the firearms were properly signed in and out.

The property store was another area of considerable sloppiness (elsewhere in the Met a chief inspector was demoted for his failure to oversee the property store at his station). Police property stores not only contain property found in the street by members of the public but also, most importantly, evidence from the scenes of crimes. They require meticulous record-keeping, which in my day was usually by an elderly police officer, but it is a post which has since been given to civilians.

Ch.Supt Grey gave me the task of sorting out the property store, which became an almost full-time job for six weeks. The previous year the Divisional Crime Squad had been stationed at West Drayton and had been responsible for trying to clear up the rampant thefts committed by the baggage handlers at Heathrow – then nicknamed 'Thiefrow'. They stole directly from luggage in the holds of aircraft but also noted the addresses on luggage labels of those going on holiday and notified their burglar friends. (To this day I never write my full address on my luggage labels.) The Divisional Crime Squad, when they made arrests, had seized suitcases full of property, none of which had been documented. Apart from contacting the officers responsible who had left the division I had to find ingenious ways of accounting for what remained. A number of large bunches of keys ended up in the station dustbin, and other more valuable items I recorded as 'property found in the street'. I remember a particularly handsome backgammon set which like other unclaimed property would later be sold at auction on behalf of the Police Widows and Orphans Fund.

A very different style of management was practised by the overall commander of the Airport Division. He was an ex-Royal Marine and full of clichés like 'don't rock the boat' and 'consume your own smoke'. If things went wrong he would find a scapegoat and never let them redeem themselves. One unfortunate chief inspector who had called an ambulance directly to a plane that had landed with a sick passenger had his promotion hopes blighted forever because the passenger had not been processed through immigration and therefore remained 'airside' and not technically in the country at all although he was in hospital.

As the superintendent at West Drayton, I was responsible for the annual appraisals of our officers, for complaints investigations and for fatal accident reports. Interviewing so many officers, I began to realise that the most demanding problems facing any manager concern unhappy staff. Many officers presented long-term problems that I was ill equipped to resolve. A very macho young man wept in my office because he had hit his wife, a long-serving PC never made any arrests because he was terrified of going to court, and there was a selfish officer, much resented by his fellows, who had booked all the summer weekends as annual leave so that he could go out with his caravan club.

The most difficult thing about dealing with complaints against police officers (mostly of rudeness or failure to take action) was not dealing with complainants or making decisions but the collation of several copies of statements and the report. I used to end with sheets of paper spread all over the floor of my office while I desperately tried to shape them into coherent files according to the strict rules for the collation of complaints. At least I did not have to do my own typing as we were blessed with a typist at West Drayton. I also found it difficult not to simply apologise to complainants as that would imply that the officer was guilty. A sincere apology would have resolved many situations.

Another more distressing task was the reading of fatal accident reports to decide whether someone should be prosecuted for causing death by dangerous driving. During my year on the Airport Division there were thirteen fatal accidents, approximately one a month, and in all but one alcohol was to blame. They did not all occur at night. Because the airport hotels had alcohol licences that allowed them to mount champagne breakfasts for business organisations, drivers could be drunk by mid-morning. One accident was caused by two young drivers racing each other along the winding roads around the airport. They were both killed. Others killed themselves running into the back of parked vehicles or mounted the pavement and killed innocent pedestrians. I rapidly became an advocate of lowering the drink-driving limit.

There were some agreeable diversions. I was sent on a week-long 'crash course' at Stanstead Airport, then semi-derelict and little used. We stayed in a guesthouse nearby where the food was excellent and watched horrifying films of aircraft disasters and were given useful advice about the strategy for dealing with crashes. The advice to put a control post upwind reminded me of an instruction I had read in a police manual about the earliest days of flying which recommended tying the plane to the nearest tree to prevent it being blown away! We learnt about square airplane windows leading to several crashes (hence why planes all now have oval windows), and about the potential of footrests for leg injuries (although they now seem to be creeping back). We also watched the Airport Fire Brigade extinguish a dramatic fire and carried out several paper exercises.

On my return to the Airport Division I decided to look at our manual of contingency plans for an aircraft crash. It was a work of art – some sixty pages of detailed but useless and impractical instructions including lists of named officers who would do the initial rescue. In a dire emergency the nearest officers have to cope, preferably with a short list of well-rehearsed instructions. These are often now printed on laminated and portable cards.

On one amusing occasion I found myself in charge of an international conference between Britain, the United States and Tanzania. It took place in one of the airport hotels and we had police snipers posted on the surrounding rooftops. My chief memory is that Julius Nyerere, President of Tanzania, and Cyrus Vance, representing the United States, were charming, speaking to and thanking us, whilst our own Foreign Secretary, David Owen, followed by a retinue of civil servants, looked neither right nor left as we stood in the corridor, and swept into the Conference Room.

After a year at West Drayton I applied for the Senior Command Course – a necessary prerequisite for the most senior ranks. The two-day extended interviews took place in a bleak and wintry Eastbourne and I had an abscess on a front tooth so was probably half-sedated. Nevertheless I was accepted but was deferred for a year due to 'lack of operational experience'. At the time it seemed unfair as many of the men going on the course were the product of recently introduced accelerated promotion schemes and had spent far fewer years on front-line police duty, but looking back I realise that I had spent a lot of time away at university and in other non-operational postings.

Initially I was to be posted to Putney, where I would have had an excellent relationship with the chief superintendent, Norman Dean, an ex-Royal Navy man, but Paddy Flynn, the DAC responsible for South East London, decided that this would not be testing enough. Instead, I was sent to Battersea where the chief superintendent was Colin Coles. So began my 'annus horribilis'.

19

BATTERSEA

I arrived at Battersea Police Station (which had a satellite station and the magistrates' court at Lavender Hill) at the beginning of 1978. The area was then on the cusp of gentrification, with a mixture of council flats and grander blocks of flats to the south of Battersea Park. Wandsworth borough had recently elected a Tory administration for the first time on a promise to cut rates. The immediate consequence was that funding for children's nurseries, the law centre, youth clubs and education had also been cut and there were some very angry people, largely from the working class, living in high-rise council flats. Their feelings were stirred up by the local press.

I was totally unprepared for the Kafkaesque situation at Battersea, where the rules of honourable behaviour were subverted and I had no one to advise me. I felt very alone and confused. I had of course known of police malpractice throughout my service but almost always at third hand through exposure in the public media. I had been shocked early in my service by stories of police officers helping themselves to cigarettes from the load of a recovered stolen lorry and also when two police officers had been arrested for shop-breaking. I was perhaps hopelessly naïve. Through newspaper accounts I also knew about the corrupt behaviour of senior detectives who had developed close relationships with the proprietors of West End clubs and belonged with them to a dedicated chapter of the Freemasons. There were also rumours about them being seen at parties with criminals such as the Richardsons and the Kray brothers and some society people who thought that gangsters were glamorous.

Some of this had been cleaned up – the Clubs Squad at West End Central had been transferred from the CID to a uniform chief inspector. There are fewer opportunities to bribe uniform police officers in this country so systemic corruption, with rare exceptions, does not develop in the uniform branches. Regular transfers, usually on promotion, also mean that patterns of corrupt behaviour are less likely to develop than among groups of officers who spend long years together. It later became policy to make all Met CID officers spend a year in uniform when they were promoted to break possible links with old associates. This policy was bitterly resented.

The public exposure of police corruption and malpractice had not prepared me for the fifteen unhappy months I spent at Battersea, which was exacerbated by the behaviour of my immediate boss, Colin Coles, and the racism, brutality and illegal behaviour of other officers.

My own direct experience of my fellow officers had been to find them generally compassionate, brave and reasonably honest, trying to do a decent job to protect the public without being too oppressive. On several occasions I had been helped in difficult situations by the kindness and common sense of fellow officers. However, there had been some blustering bullies among my senior officers and some constables who allegedly took pleasure in teasing vagrants. One of the police drivers at Kings Cross would deliberately drive at flocks of pigeons in the roadway just to upset me (they were always too canny to be hit) but this was confined to an individual and was not widespread or systemic.

My experiences at Battersea were to be very different. The chief superintendent, Colin Coles, was a tall and good-looking man who allegedly had a good reputation for dealing with public order events. However, I soon learned that there was a history to this man, who was both feared and hated by his officers. He had spent eight years (a surprisingly long time) as a chief inspector at Rochester Row Police Station. Gradually I was told stories about the acts of revenge that had been meted out to him there. Someone had defecated in his uniform hat, and, more imaginatively, during one night duty they had taken his bicycle to pieces and strung every nut, bolt and spoke on strings around the police station, which must have made him very angry.

Initially my impressions were favourable – although his manner was chilly he seemed calm and organised and he was very sentimental about his twelve-year-old daughter (he had two divorces behind him). I only began to have doubts about his character and his passion for disciplining officers when one evening in my first few weeks there he took me to sit in a car to keep observation on a pub where he believed officers were drinking after licensing hours. This was wholly inappropriate for officers of our rank and should have been dealt with at inspector level, but clearly he did not trust them. Moreover, I noticed that he was visibly excited – his face was flushed – at the prospect of catching some officers in a disciplinary offence. Fortunately, the station grapevine had worked well – the pub closed on time and no officers emerged.

Another main problem for me was the excessive consumption of alcohol. Senior officers then had an entertainment allowance and generally had a drinks cupboard so that they could offer hospitality to visitors. It was also the practice to encourage detective officers to spend time in pubs to cultivate (sometimes mythical) informants. The heavy drinking sessions at Battersea were held in Colin Coles' office, with the CID and uniform chief inspectors in attendance, and each was expected to bring a bottle of spirits. I rapidly opted out of these social evenings, which surely didn't endear me to Colin Coles, but I had to drive home anyhow. The detective chief inspector was an incompetent old sweat who told me that he did not 'like women on the squad because they would not tell lies on oath'! Some years later he was arrested for drink-driving when he tried to say that his wife had been in the driving seat. The uniform chief inspector became a friend, but I was concerned for him because he had a blackout after one of these drinking sessions and spent the night unconscious in his office.

I was given assignments which were beyond my knowledge and experience, although they would have been appropriate for my rank with helpful advice. I suspect that Colin Coles, who was undoubtedly jealous of my selection for the Senior Command Course, hoped that I would come unstuck, as indeed I did. He offered me no assistance. One such assignment was the opening of a nightclub by Roddy Llewellyn Jones, then Princess Margaret's boyfriend. He had converted a derelict building in Battersea Square, which is now a smart location, and was having a gala opening for all his rich socialite friends. We did not anticipate any problems and had about fifteen officers with a sergeant and inspector in actual charge and me in notional command. To our horror, as we deployed our officers on the narrow pavements around the entrance to the nightclub we found an angry mob stirred up by the local press who shouted and spat at the smart guests as they arrived elegantly attired in long gowns and evening clothes. We really did not have enough officers to contain the crowd and keep space on the pavement. I considered sending for reinforcements, but the splendid inspector, who had a tall and commanding presence, managed to control the situation until the last of the guests were safely inside and the crowd dispersed. It was one occasion when I wished I was a six-foot man. For some weeks afterwards I expected there to be an official complaint, but none transpired.

More serious were my travails with the CID and the two complaints I was given to investigate. There had been a spate of robberies on the buses that ran between Brixton and Battersea, and the CID at Lavender Hill had developed a practice of arresting black youths, whether or not evidence justified it, and leaving them in the cells at Lavender Hill for two or three days in the hopes they would confess. Quite apart from this denial of human rights, illegality and the worsening of already fraught relationships with the black community, I was very sorry for the uniform station sergeants who were technically responsible for the prisoners. It was this type of behaviour that led soon after to the introduction of PACE (the Police and Criminal Evidence Act). When I objected to the detective inspector I was later visited by the detective chief superintendent, who asked me in the presence of Colin Coles if I was soft on criminals. I felt intimidated and found it very difficult to reply coherently.

My most serious downfall concerned my investigation of two official complaints – both by black men. One had been arrested by three Crime Squad officers. (There is a dangerous tendency in the police service, whenever there is serious problem, to set up a squad of officers who rapidly develop an elitist mentality and standards of conduct that are outside the usual norms and often illegal.) One of the three officers had come into the cell where the man was detained and had hit him so severely that he had a broken jaw which required surgery and still showed a scar when I interviewed him some months later. He did not know which of the three arresting officers had hit him, and I knew that they would never stand on an identification parade, so, probably foolishly, I arranged that he and his solicitor would sit in the crowded foyer of the magistrates' court when I knew the three officers would be present for another case. He had no doubt which of the three constables had hit him – it was a big, burly young man – and pointed him out to me and his solicitor. The consequence was that I was accused of unfairly demoralising a hard-working young officer. The complaint was handed over to another, more compliant officer, and was eventually discontinued for 'lack of evidence'.

The other complaint came from a black man who had repeatedly been stopped when driving his car. He was arrested on three separate occasions, although never charged with any offence. This was less traumatic, but it was difficult to make headway as there were more than thirty witnesses, many of whom were on long-term sick leave or otherwise absent. My failure to complete this enquiry in a reasonable time was another reason why, for the first time in my service, I received an adverse annual report. I had a difficult appraisal interview with the divisional commander (a pleasant but rather ineffectual man, chiefly memorable for believing that no police car should be allowed to exceed the speed limit), who was embarrassed by the situation. I was terrified that he might recommend that I did not go on the Senior Command Course, which would have ended all my future career prospects. I found myself obsessing constantly about my experiences at Battersea and going over and over the ways in which I might have behaved differently or even how I might revenge myself on Colin Coles.

My only moment of mild amusement at Battersea was when I looked at the division's contingency plans for flooding. Battersea lies below sea level, and before the erection of the Thames Barrier there would have been serious problems if the river had 'overtopped' the banks. The plans, like those for disasters at Heathrow, turned out to be a lovingly prepared and detailed sixty-page document full of contradictory instructions. For example, there were two essential priority actions – one was to move all the station documents to the top floor and the other was to knock up all those living in basement or ground-floor flats. I imagine sensible instructions for emergencies are now computerised and available on smartphones.

In the spring of 1979, I escaped and went back to Bramshill for the six-month Senior Command Course. I had not entirely escaped from Colin Coles, who later turned up at Hounslow as deputy to the commander, but he no longer troubled me as we were of equal rank. In due course, to my great pleasure, I outranked him when I became a commander.

20

SENIOR COMMAND COURSE AND CHISWICK

I arrived at Bramshill in the spring of 1979 for the Senior Command Course feeling depressed and cynical about the police service. Unusually, I was not looking forward to spending time at the Police College, and during the course I wrote a bitter essay about police management that my tutor thought was much too negative.

I was of course the only woman on the course of twenty students, but I was used to that situation and got on companionably with my fellow officers. Many women have since achieved chief officer rank, including several chief constables and currently the splendid Commissioner of the Metropolitan Police, Cressida Dick, but forty years ago I was a rarity. Many of my fellow students went on to become chief constables. Bill Taylor, with whom I shared bathroom facilities and whom I teased about his personal supply of toilet paper, went on to be a distinguished Commissioner of the City of London. Most of them were younger than I, had less service and had come through graduate entry or other accelerated promotion schemes. These were not available when I joined, so I decided that most of the differences in age and experience were probably due to my bad timing rather than gender bias!

We had interesting exercises on policing public order or other major incidents and carried out joint exercises with the military. We had an agreeable weekend at Latimer – a military centre in an old mansion where we were served meals by young soldiers wearing white gloves. We played croquet on the lawn against a military team; much to the surprise of our class-conscious hosts, we won – partly due to my prowess at the game. This was very satisfactory as we felt we were being patronised. I enjoyed noticing the tribal differences between the three services as we discussed various scenarios (nuclear war, major disasters) and possible courses of action.

The army officers seemed eccentric in their varied regimental uniforms, including tartan trousers, the RAF officers were humourless and rule-bound technicians (essential if responsible for flying highly complex aircraft), and on the whole we found the Royal Navy officers most like ourselves, fun to be with and pragmatic in their approach to solving problems.

We also had attachments in small groups to other forces. I spent a few days with the Devon and Cornwall Constabulary where the chief constable was John Alderson, whom I knew from my time on the staff when he had been commandant at the Police College. He was introducing a system of neighbourhood policing that involved much closer liaison with the county councils and police authority, although the police service has always been very suspicious of any form of political control. We went to a meeting of the police authority where I was surprised by his apparent subservience to their views and also saw for the first time the problems of accountability to politicians and the fraught question of who has ultimate control. The police service felt strongly that politicians should not be in control as this could lead to political bias, but politicians felt that an independent police service was undemocratic. The Met had moved some way towards political accountability when we first aligned our divisional boundaries with those of the London boroughs (inefficiently, court and coroner boundaries in London are still unaligned) and had occasional joint meetings with local councillors, who often surprised me by their ignorance. The MP at Battersea, for example, thought we had hundreds of officers to deploy on his streets. Unlike in the rest of the country, the Home Office was the only police authority for the Metropolitan Police, and I thought then that it should be counter-balanced by some more local control.

The members of the course were dispatched to various foreign countries, and I spent an agreeable five days at the French Police Training Academy at Lyon with three colleagues. We had an outing to Toulon through the lavender fields in full flower and were astonished by the inadequacy of their forensic science laboratory, which was little more than a dark cupboard with a few test tubes. (Many years later, in 1993, I was a member of a House of Lords Committee that looked at our forensic science system and recommended that it should not be privatised – which has subsequently happened, and of course turned out to be disastrous.) Despite our interesting few days in France in 1979, the French judicial system is so different from ours, with a civilian administrator taking charge at major incidents, and the split between the Gendarmerie in the countryside and the Police Nationale in the cities, that it was difficult to draw any lessons for our report. We were surprised to find they kept secret files on all their politicians but were impressed by their provision of 'foyers' as a resort that offered facilities and counselling for young offenders.

In the autumn of 1979, I was posted to Chiswick. I was to spend the next three years here, first as superintendent and then as chief superintendent (unusual, as one is generally moved on promotion). Chiswick is a largely middle-class and prosperous part of London with tree-lined streets and substantial houses in single occupancy, although one in Chiswick High Road was occupied by Erin Pizzey's Women's Shelter, where we occasionally had problems with drunken and aggressive husbands.

The other half of the ground was Brentford, where we had a satellite police station managed by a chief inspector and which was quite different in character. Although there was a pocket of gentility in Isleworth, there were two large council estates with high-rise blocks. The Green Dragon Estate had won an architectural award but its design created particular problems. The underground car park was a hidden haven for car thieves, and the flats all had hatches for milk bottles that were so flimsy that children could easily and regularly break in to the flats. The other large estate – the Ivybridge Estate – had tall white tower blocks that are a distinctive landmark to be seen from the left-hand side of the plane when about to land at Heathrow.

The other main focus for policing on the division was Brentford Football Club, where I spent many Saturday afternoons standing on the terraces with freezing feet watching rather indifferent games of football. The crowd in those days was rarely more than 6,000 and we had little trouble. We usually managed with a single serial of twenty PCs under the command of an inspector and chief inspector and were congratulated on having the lowest police-to-crowd ratio in London. However, even the most well-behaved crowd can become overexcited and some young officers were affected by the noise and possibly by media hype about hooliganism. I saw a young officer in tears one day, and on another occasion managed to halt one who had taken out his truncheon and was about to wade into a minor scuffle.

There were occasions when we had visiting teams which required more serious measures of crowd control. Some were due to the myths of past problems. Whenever Reading came to Brentford, someone at the pre-match briefing would remind the officers that on one occasion a hand-grenade had been thrown onto the pitch. When I researched this it turned out to have been in 1948 and the grenade had not exploded. Cup ties were a particular problem. When Millwall, whose supporters had an evil reputation, came to Brentford we had assistance from other divisions and a serious number of officers both inside and outside the ground. One match where we had not anticipated trouble was a cup tie against a small non-league team who came accompanied by hordes of overexcited children and teenagers who ran about the terraces in a thoroughly disorganised fashion. We were more used to fans who were largely self-policing.

Managing the division was not difficult as I was supported by generally excellent staff such as the admin sergeant who ran the section dealing with traffic summonses (not easy as we had three separate court areas to deal with) as well as all the station records of sickness, annual reports and records of liquor licences, shotgun certificates and statistical returns required by Scotland Yard. He also, because of these multifarious tasks, knew where problems were emerging and would drop me a quiet word. When I first arrived at Chiswick my immediate boss was an ineffectual chief superintendent on the point of retirement, so even before

I was promoted to take his place I was effectively doing all the day-to-day management. I also had an excellent chief inspector who had served in the army in the Korean War and was a sound source of practical advice and an ever-present support at football matches. (He was much later arrested for allegedly vandalising a telephone box outside his house on the A30 which was regularly used as a urinal by passing lorry drivers, but the case was dismissed at court due to the lack of crucial evidence – the Post Office staff keeping watch had not actually seen him entering the box.)

The main problems of management were those met in most organisations. What does one do about the alcoholic officer who will not seek help? Is that person with a bad sickness record malingering, or do they have some undisclosed illness? How does one change attitudes or introduce new procedures? However, some exterior events affected our fairly tranquil division. This was the time of the IRA bombing campaign in London, and we had contingency plans for dealing with bomb alerts. Even so, my officers sometimes responded irrationally. When there was bombing in central London, my station officer rushed out and closed the yard gates – a futile gesture as Chiswick Police Station is a glass-fronted modern building on the High Street. After the Brixton riots in 1981, however, some of my officers were more directly affected – some slept badly and had nightmares for many months afterwards. One officer wore the police trousers that were then made of man-made fibre and had all the hairs on his legs burnt off and was lucky to escape serious burns. One of my best Home Beat officers, PC Smooker, had found himself in a smaller riot in west London and lay on the ground thinking he was going to be killed. He was very shaken for some months afterwards.

At this time, David McNee was the Commissioner of the Met. The Home Office had allegedly considered the heads of the two largest forces in the country, Philip Knights in the West Midlands and David McNee in Strathclyde. They had allegedly plumped for him because his force was introducing a computerised Command and Control system. He was, however, a man out of his depth in the Met. He had one meeting (a previously annual event) with all his senior officers, and because they argued with him he cancelled all future meetings. Under Robert Mark the force had begun to take some tentative steps towards greater openness and accountability, but this was now shut down and we were not allowed to talk to the press. When I met some of the local residents who wanted a permanent police presence in their road to stop it being used as a rat-run I was not allowed to say how few officers I had on foot patrol in the streets at any one time – usually only four or five for the whole division – and I certainly could not spare one for a quiet residential road. (The road has now had bollards and chicanes introduced to slow the traffic.)

David McNee lost all credibility in the force after the Brixton riots. He had previously issued an instruction that more senior officers should patrol the streets in uniform (Colin Coles responded by walking the several miles in uniform from Battersea to Wandsworth to see the divisional commander). After the Brixton riots had died down, McNee was seen on television being shown round the streets of Brixton in plainclothes.

I had some operational experiences. I was fairly regularly woken in the night for permission to issue firearms. Fortunately, none of these led to serious incidents. I was also responsible at one armed siege. One of the game wardens for Richmond Park, who had several guns for deer-culling, had been rejected by his girlfriend and had become drunk and was seen on the doorstep of his bungalow waving a gun about and shouting that he was going to kill her or himself. By the time I arrived at the scene he was inside the house, all was quiet and the armed officers were keeping an armed vigil. I was just in time to seize a young detective glassy-eyed with adrenalin who was apparently intent on storming the house alone. After nothing had happened for a while, one of the armed officers went up to a window and saw that the man was lying in an armchair, apparently passed out, so we went in and he was arrested and all his guns were seized. It was a very sad case as he was obviously going to lose his job, his tied house as well as his girlfriend. Oddly, what I found particularly poignant was the lively blue macaw that was in his kitchen and that we fed with peanuts.

Towards the end of my time at Chiswick things became more difficult. The new superintendent, Roger Barr, my deputy, had a reputation as an expert on public order. He had been a boxing blue at Oxford and was a keen rugger player and athlete. However, I don't think he found it easy to have a woman as his boss and his need for regular amounts of alcohol began to affect the whole station. We had been a totally alcohol-free zone beforehand. One day after Roger arrived I found a CID officer who was typing a report with a can of beer by his side and I made it clear that it was totally unacceptable. From early in my service it had been drummed into us that 'drinking on duty' was a disciplinary offence. I had had great qualms early in my service one Christmas at accepting a small glass of sherry from a lonely old lady. Drink had become a problem in the force until David McNee issued an instruction in 1978 saying there should be no alcohol on police premises.

Roger liked to go to a pub at lunchtime, and after meetings with the young officers in the crime squad he would take them out for a drinking session at the end of which one young policeman was found up to his knees in mud on the Brentford foreshore. The policing of Brentford's football matches became much more dramatic as he introduced dog patrols and mounted officers. However, I was much more concerned about his habit of drinking with the directors before and during a match. I had always kept them at arm's length because I knew that they fiddled gate numbers and the extent of their profits for tax purposes. The turnstiles, which were used to count numbers, could allow more than one person through at a time, so reducing the apparent numbers at a match and the club's tax liability. Roger would not listen to my advice and our relationship became frosty. After I left Chiswick, things came to a head and he was posted as commandant to the Cadet School, where presumably there would be fewer temptations and his athletic prowess could be put to good use.

One of my most traumatic experiences whilst at Chiswick was attending the scene of a fire where a mother and child had been burnt to death. Her husband had escaped by jumping through a window. The sight of their half-melted bodies came back to me in flashbacks for a long time afterwards. We had three murders during my three years at Chiswick. One was an unremarkable 'domestic' except that the couple were male homosexuals. One was a burglary that went wrong; the victim was an elderly woman and the perpetrator was a youth well known to the police at Brentford. The third was initially more puzzling. A young girl claimed that her boyfriend had been stabbed in the street by a gang of youths. She received a great deal of sympathy until after several days she admitted that it was she who had stabbed him.

At this point in 1982 my career took a turn for the better. Ken Newman had been appointed as commissioner and was full of new ideas. Graduate police officers suddenly found themselves valued and were scooped up to run his various new schemes. I was appointed to run one of his planning groups at New Scotland Yard (although I was notionally posted to a slot in the Traffic Department).

21

PLANNING GROUP

I thoroughly enjoyed my twelve months running one of Ken Newman's Planning Groups as I had no managerial responsibilities and could give free rein to my imagination. Ken Newman was an energetic and inspirational Commissioner who believed in innovation. It was a great contrast to the stultifying regime of his predecessor, David McNee, who had closed down communication with journalists and could not cope with contrary viewpoints. Because the force had to find a slot for me in the number of chief superintendents permitted by the Home Office to be at headquarters, I was notionally responsible for B2 Branch of the Traffic Department and so formally had an office on the south side of the river in Tintagel House near the MI6 building. This branch consisted of an inspector and two sergeants whose job was to try and ease the flow of London's traffic by encouraging the gas, water and electricity companies to synchronise their roadworks. They were also responsible for planning the movement of mobile cranes and other outsize vehicles. I knew nothing about these matters so there was little that I could contribute.

My real job was in a tiny room in New Scotland Yard where I had a team of three bright young officers with academic qualifications. We were charged with looking at the service's paperwork and administrative systems with a view to eliminating waste. We managed to rid the force of a number of forms and administrative tasks, but it was not nearly enough. When I joined there were hundreds of specific forms for different tasks such as reporting accidents, traffic offences, lost property, lost dogs and missing children. Witness statements, for example, were taken on form 992, with continuation sheets on form 991. Police stations also had to produce regular reports and statistics which served no useful purpose. At Chiswick, for example, we were supposed to keep an impossibly up-to-date list of people who owned small boats in case there was serious flooding of the River Thames – another overly complex plan that would not have been useful in a real emergency. I had decided not to spend my scarce resources of manpower on such a task.

Among the tasks and forms we managed to eliminate were the licences for pedlars and hawkers – only one had been issued in the past three years, and we recommended that this should be a matter for local authorities, although I suspect the procedure just ceased to exist. One of our great successes was to invent a formula for the provision of personal radios to officers. Home Office stinginess meant that in comparison to other police forces we were woefully undersupplied, and did not have enough radios at police stations to cover our needs. Our radios were constantly breaking down, and the workshops could only mend them by cannibalising spare parts from other radios – thus diminishing supplies even further. We mischievously invented an elaborate formula based on the numbers of uniform and CID officers at each station, shift patterns and time required to recharge the batteries. This so baffled the Home Office that they finally granted a considerable increase in personal radios.

Whilst we were dealing with these fairly straightforward tasks, one of Ken Newman's bright young chief inspectors, Tony Burns-Howell, who had studied management at the City University, was attempting a wholesale change in police culture by introducing management jargon to the Met. Thus in the early 1990s we were suddenly expected to have mission statements and to fill reams of paper with aims, objectives, tasks, action plans, signposts and outcomes. Just as my group was trying to simplify things and reduce paperwork, Tony was introducing new layers of complexity. In irritation I wrote a Gilbert and Sullivan parody which began:

> If you're anxious for to shine
> In the new objective line
> As a man of action plans
> You must learn the teeming herds
> Of fashionable words
> Like environmental scans.
> You must network pretty mazes
> And discourse in novel phrases
> Of your complex state of mind.

Although this alleviated my ire somewhat it was of course not published, and we were haunted by the need for action plans and mission statements for some years thereafter. At the end of twelve months I passed a promotion board and was promoted to commander and thus joined the nationwide ranks of chief officers.

I was the only woman commander in the Met at that time. Many women have since progressed much further, but at the time I was a rarity. I was often the only woman when I attended annual conferences of all the chief constables and their assistants, but this had the advantage that everyone knew me and I was treated with respect.

As commander, I was posted to a position in New Scotland Yard in the A (for Administration) Department, where I was to spend the next three years responsible for a heterogeneous collection of six branches – Courts, Deportation, Firearms, Obscene Publications, Coroners' Officers and the Neighbourhood Policing Project.

22

COMMANDER

I was very much looking forward to the two great privileges of joining the ranks of chief officer in the Met: a dedicated car and driver (a luxury long since abolished), and a mounted policing course (so that theoretically I could take charge from horseback at public order events). I was never sent on a mounted course and was constantly fobbed off by my immediate boss, Colin Dinsdale, with feeble excuses (probably on instruction from Assistant Commissioner Maclean, a pleasant but reactionary man in charge of public order events) when I pressed for an explanation. I was irritated by this evidence of sexism, especially as the riding school was only fifteen minutes' drive from my house and I like horses.

It was clear that my gender was the problem, but no one would admit it! There were already a large number of women in the 200-strong Mounted Branch, and many of them were on duty at public order events. Some years before I had been a member of a working group with the Equal Opportunities Commission looking at sexual discrimination in the Met. As a result of its recommendations, many previously closed specialisms in the CID, traffic patrols (one of the best area car fast-response drivers at Chiswick when I was there had been a woman), dog handling and the Mounted Branch had been opened up to women. There was a particular problem for the Mounted Branch as applications by women outnumbered the men by ten to one. A much more salient problem was the troubled relationship that the Met had (and still has) with the black and ethnic minorities of London, but there was no such examination of racial discrimination within the Met. This struck me as odd and horrifying after my experiences at Battersea and remembering my research on race relations at Manchester University.

My car and driver, however, were a delight. My driver, Harry Ball, looked after me like a father for the eight years that I was a commander. He had been a regular soldier and had had bad experiences with other senior officers, so it was a tentative relationship to begin with, but we became a team. He was unfailingly punctual and I soon came to know his wife and daughters. He was an enthusiastic keeper of koi carp, helped with my fish pond, and was a brilliant woodworker. I am constantly reminded of him by my garden bench and my spice rack. Alas, soon after we both retired he died of lung cancer – he was an inveterate smoker, although never in the car.

My responsibilities at the Yard were a curious collection of branches. Some were major responsibilities, like the Courts Department, which oversaw the policing of all Magistrates' and Coroners' Courts in the Metropolitan area. At Chiswick we had had to deal with three separate Magistrates' Courts, all with different paperwork and procedures which they jealously guarded. None had common boundaries with police or local authorities – still an unresolved problem – but otherwise since courts operated as largely autonomous units it entailed little work for me whilst I was at the Yard except the occasional meeting with the Magistrates' Association.

More problematic was the Obscene Publications Branch, run by a chief inspector and a principal, a senior civil servant. The superintendent who had previously been in charge had become much too close to Mary Whitehouse and her Viewers' and Listeners' Association and their campaigns against pornography. They had sponsored a lecture trip for him to Australia. Mary Whitehouse invited me to lunch at the Carlton Club in the hope of recruiting me to her cause, and I went, having obtained clearance from Colin Dinsdale, my boss. I enjoyed the lunch with several of her supporters and was amused to see inside that grand bastion of Tory privilege, but I had no further contact with her or her association, and I suspect she thought my views were too liberal.

A major problem in the Obscene Publications Branch was the effect that constantly reading and viewing pornography was having on the staff. One of the mature officers said it made having sex with his wife difficult, and I was particularly concerned that much of the reading of potentially pornographic magazines and books was being done by very young male clerical staff. I tried without success to suggest to the senior civil servant in charge that mature women would be better able to cope. He was later replaced by a woman, and changes were made. My own policy was that sex between consenting adults, however outlandish, was acceptable, but anything involving children (or animals) should be pursued with the utmost vigour. With the advent of the internet it has become much harder to set guidelines of what is acceptable and how children can be protected.

Other branches for which I was notionally responsible were Firearms Licensing (entirely run by civil staff who knew far more about the subject than I did, although I had signed many shotgun certificates when at Chiswick) and the Deportation Group (not as controversial then as they have later become when staffed by Group 4 and others) but my major interest and consumer of time and energy was the Neighbourhood Policing Project, which was described as the 'largest experiment in action research in Europe'.

The Neighbourhood Policing Project was an experiment set up in the wake of the Brixton riots and the Scarman report's recommendations. It was an attempt to improve relations with the black, especially West Indian, community, and to reduce and detect crime. It was run by two bright graduate chief inspectors, Jim Hart and Ian Beckett, who were full of the latest ideas about both sociology and computer technology.

As originally conceived by this duo and sold to the commissioner, the idea was that different measures would be introduced at three of the most racially sensitive and crime-ridden divisions in the Met – Brixton, Kilburn and Notting Hill – with Hackney acting as a control. This idea built on the splendid work of Alec Marnoch, the commander at Brixton, who had established a comprehensive system of neighbourhood policing with dedicated constables and outreach programmes to youth clubs and other organisations. A similar scheme was to be introduced at Notting Hill with the latest computerised technology to look at crime trends and patterns, and Kilburn was to receive just the assistance of computer technology.

Unfortunately, by the time I was responsible for the project it had been hopelessly compromised. The commissioner's impatience (and lack of understanding of scientific method) meant that all four of these divisions had been made to introduce both neighbourhood policing schemes and computer technology before my arrival. This meant that there was no way of evaluating the effectiveness of the scheme as no database had been established at the start. However, I was very enthusiastic about the philosophy of community policing that underlay the scheme and of the use of computers (which had advanced a long way since my time in Management Services six or seven years earlier) and I spent a lot of time visiting the various stations and the project team who were based in Putney. A half-hearted attempt was made by the Home Office to establish the cost-effectiveness of the scheme, but with no standards of comparison and the flawed assumption that everything can be given a price it was a failure – much as I expected.

My other problem was the excessive enthusiasm of my two chief inspectors. Ian was a charismatic speaker and constantly oversold the project to fellow police officers, who subsequently became cynical and disillusioned when no miracle occurred. Ian also kept having new ideas, like 'conflict resolution', to tack onto the original project. When Ian Beckett moved on from the project his office staff gave him a copy of Machiavelli's *The Prince*! Jim Hart was a much more earnest and hard-working young man who did his best in difficult circumstances. I gave him a very good annual report.

Towards the end of my time at Scotland Yard I found myself responsible for the running of the Control Centre that was coordinating the National Police response to the miners' strike. It had already been in existence for some months, so mine was a purely formal responsibility for an organisation about which I had deep misgivings. I was appalled by the assumption of the government, and particularly Margaret Thatcher, that the police service should be used in partisan fashion. The whole ethos of the police service in this country has been to act 'without fear or favour' and not to take sides. The Prime Minister's reference to 'our police' and 'thin blue lines' was particularly distasteful to me as she placed the police service on one side of a political divide.

Many police officers came from mining families, and others behaved disgracefully (boasting of their enhanced overtime payments, for example), resulting in long-term alienation and bitterness in Yorkshire and Lancashire. Although I accepted the necessity for coordination of police activity, I also disliked the fact that every morning an arrogant man from the Cabinet Office would come to obtain the latest war report as though the Government were in charge and we were conducting a battle on their behalf.

After three interesting and enjoyable years at Scotland Yard I was posted out to the newly formed north-west slice of London as one of DAC Richard Wells' two deputies. All through my service London has been sliced up in different ways. Each incoming commissioner thinks that the Met's problems (like those of the National Health Service) are purely structural. Management consultants have made fortunes from their recommendations about different structures. When I first joined, there were four areas in each corner of London, all of them containing several divisions and a well-appointed sports ground. The consultants pointed out that the areas merely acted as postboxes for correspondence going to the Yard, and they were abolished. (With them too went the delightful custom that when their commanders inspected the station books they counter-signed in green ink whereas chief superintendents' signatures were in red.) Then we had our borders aligned with those of the London boroughs. Then, finally, there was the central egg and seven slices of cake, and chief inspector stations were abolished.

We were accommodated in what had been the Police Section House (living quarters for single officers) at Kingsbury, and I was responsible for Welfare, Administration and Complaints (a role suitable for a woman?). We had been allocated almost no staff or resources, and it was very unclear where the lines of responsibility lay between ourselves and the various chief superintendents running their divisions. It was an additional frustration that Richard Wells had (rather like John Alderson at the Police College) an idealised view of management where no decision could be made until all were in agreement. In consequence we had long and exhausting meetings with our chief superintendents because one or two were never going to agree to what they saw as newfangled ideas. My fellow commander, who was responsible for Public Order and other operational matters (including the policing of Wembley Stadium), eventually had a nervous breakdown because of the lack of clarity and because he was blamed when things went wrong. I was present at Wembley for the last of the Calcutta Cup football matches between England and Scotland. The fans had been drinking all morning and the scenes of disorder were such that the fixture was never repeated. I saw numerous drunken scuffles, but there were no serious injuries. Fortunately, my role was only to advise on health and safety issues so I was not involved in the actual policing. I nonetheless pointed out to some of the administrators the hazards of half-completed building works with broken reinforcing rods and lumps of concrete that could be used as weapons.

Although I was not directly responsible for the CID, they also had their problems. In particular there was a prolonged battle with the Crown Prosecution Service, and I joined the chief inspector in the discussions, because the CPS would not prosecute a group of youths who had kicked to death another young man. Their objection was that the CPS lawyer said he could not determine which of them had left the imprint of his boot in the victim's fractured skull. The detective chief inspector and I were horrified by the decision as we felt that they should all stand trial as some measure of solace to the young man's family and a public demonstration of their guilt, even if they were subsequently acquitted.

The CID also uncovered and prosecuted a paedophile ring but, although they knew the tentacles spread far beyond our slice of London, they were not allowed by the Yard to investigate further on the grounds of 'lack of resources' – in view of the latest revelations this was a short-sighted decision, but before the introduction of modern technology, surveillance and evidence gathering took a lot of man (or woman) power.

After two years at Kingsbury I failed my first promotion board for DAC rank, which was not a surprise as two excellent young men from outside the Met were selected – Wynn Jones from Thames Valley and Paul Condon, who was later to become commissioner – so I did not feel particularly downcast. I was then posted to take charge of all Met training at the great complex at Hendon with its sports grounds, cadet school and CID as well as recruit training. I was also notionally responsible for dog and horse training.

23

HENDON

My failure at my first promotion board for the rank of deputy assistant commissioner was not very surprising or upsetting because it was not unusual to fail first time (although I had never failed a selection board before) and because the two men who were selected were both highly regarded officers. I was, however, annoyed that I discovered the outcome through an overheard conversation in the lift at New Scotland Yard. That rankled. I have always tried to tell my officers who have failed promotion boards before the much more agreeable task of congratulating those who have succeeded.

Although I felt I was being side-lined into an administrative posting rather than a front-line role that would have been better for my chances of promotion (and perhaps training was seen as a more suitable posting for a woman?), my responsibilities at Hendon were considerable. They included the Mounted Branch riding school at Imber Court, the dog handlers' training centre and the CID school. These largely acted as autonomous units, and both dogs and horses were located elsewhere, so my primary focus was on the initial five-month course for all recruits and their subsequent classes whilst they were still on probation. It was a time of buoyant recruitment, so there were nearly 2,000 officers to be taught the basics of powers of arrest and how to deal with a variety of taxing situations such as street accidents and mental illness.

I was also an enthusiastic supporter of the Cadet School based at Hendon, which I saw as a public service and a way of enhancing our recruitment of ethnic minorities and other young girls and boys who had struggled with their education. Junior cadets joined at fifteen and in addition to general education had great opportunities to show leadership and develop confidence in sport and adventure training. Senior cadets spent some time at police stations and learning skills such as first aid (all police officers then had certificates from the St John Ambulance service). I was sad when the Cadet School was deemed an unnecessary luxury due to a surfeit of adult police recruits and abolished towards the end of my service, thus losing a great way of providing opportunities for children from disadvantaged backgrounds.

On the whole my duties were fairly routine and administrative and I had very supportive staff. However, there were occasional emergencies. I was responsible for sacking one potential recruit before he had even been sworn in! He was an ex-soldier and had seen service in Malaysia. He had spent the Sunday night in the accommodation block, and first thing on the Monday morning a greatly perturbed sergeant came into my office and said that this man had been showing his fellow and very young recruits photographs of a British soldier holding the severed heads of two Malays. The photos were horrifying. After consultation with the federation sergeant I agreed that he should be sacked forthwith. There were no repercussions.

Otherwise, basic training followed a regular routine with a new intake of recruits each month and was much like the training I had endured, although as it lasted five months rather than thirteen weeks there were more opportunities for discussion and less rote learning of powers of arrest. Also, the introduction of personal radios had made it much easier to send for help so there was less need for individual initiative.

More problematic than the basic recruit training were the courses we ran for sergeants and inspectors in an attempt to introduce new ideas and attitudes. Much of it was 'race relations' training, which was often resented by older officers who disliked the implicit criticism of their behaviour. The courses were often delivered by outside consultants who were seen as patronising and ignorant of police work. One great success in this area was that half a dozen of the training school staff went on a course which included the total immersion of staying with a black or Asian family. This had a profound and positive effect. We also had a variety of external consultants who charged exorbitant fees, many hundreds of pounds, for a day's work and administered trite personality questionnaires to students on the inspector course to determine their management styles. Of far greater use and gravitas was a retired colonel from the Army Education Corps who helped drag some of our training methods into the twentieth century by using computers and distance learning (now a commonplace).

One of the great problems for the police service is the incessant flow of new legislation as politicians like to show that they have thought up new ways of tackling crime. Retraining also takes up an inordinate amount of police time. For example, the Data Protection Act entailed all 26,000 Met police officers going on a five-day course on a matter that seemed abstruse and irrelevant. When I joined in 1956, almost all crimes were covered by two Acts of Parliament that were almost a century old: the Offences Against the Person Act 1861 and the Offences Against Property Act 1861. Since then there has been a deluge of legislation redefining larceny as theft and burglary as breaking and entering, among other things. The consequence was that we had a team of six officers at Hendon trying to understand the intentions of legislators and converting new Acts of Parliament into comprehensible chunks for police instruction manuals.

This task is not easy, as I have observed since in the House of Lords. Legislation is often vague and self-contradictory, and does nothing to address the root causes of crime, which are often rooted in a lack of youth services and educational and social opportunities. Early in my time in the House of Lords I made a rather frivolous speech saying there were too many barristers in Parliament who only know about serious crime and villains and know nothing about the vast quantity of more ordinary crimes and their perpetrators. To deal with these would require much greater investment in education and the social services, which would of course require adequate funding, which politicians see as unpopular with the voting public. In the short term it might mean higher taxes, but in the long run it could reduce expenditure on prisons and the police service.

I did have one tangle with police bureaucracy at this time. I had thought for a long time that the generous provision to the police service of sports clubs, playing fields, gymnasia and swimming pools should be viewed as a public asset and open to schools and sports clubs. I was horrified when I arrived at Hendon to find that the splendid new swimming pool had been deliberately built to dimensions a little too short for international practice. When I was at Chiswick I had tried to make the little-used gym in the Section House open to local schools but had failed. On the campus at Hendon there were vast empty playing fields that were rarely occupied, and I tried again but was told that 'Treasury rules would not permit it'. No one was ever able to tell me the exact nature of those rules.

Whilst at Hendon I had my second board for DAC rank and failed again. Unlike my first board, where the two men selected were rising young stars, the five men selected from my second board were all Met officers who lacked my experience and qualifications but possessed social ties, such as being ex-Royal Marines or rugby players, with members of the board. Of course, at the top of an organisation where people have served together for many years it is personal relationships that count. I had hoped that the presiding commissioner, Peter Imbert, an old friend from my Police College days, would weigh in my favour.

I was bitter and resentful, but when I complained about the injustice to one of my two chief superintendents at Hendon he told me not to make such a fuss. I sharply said to him, 'Don't be so patronising' and was surprised to see tears of hurt in his eyes. He thought he was advising me for my own good. This was one of the few occasions on which I had been directly affected by gender discrimination. I was more amused on another occasion by a visit from John Patten MP, who was a Minister of State at the Home Office and must have been inadequately briefed. I assembled all my senior officers in my office to greet him and he, assuming that the senior officer would be a man, looked at all the men in turn. They became increasingly embarrassed, shuffling their feet, and eventually pushed him in my direction.

Towards the end of my service things took an unexpected turn for the better. Ted Mitchell, my immediate boss, who had passed the board for DAC that I had most recently failed, broke his shoulder and I was appointed Acting DAC in the Personnel Department for eight months in his place. I had held a meeting with him a few weeks earlier when he had to conduct my annual review, which had been difficult for both of us. He was visibly embarrassed. The assistant commissioner, Wynn Jones, who was in charge of Personnel and Training, was one of the two bright young men who had succeeded on my first board. He came to the Met from Thames Valley and, apart from his views on the Greenham Common women, whom he called 'slags', we got on very well. He was full of radical ideas like abolishing the height restrictions for police officers and replacing them with tests of physical fitness. This meant, he said, we could recruit ex-Gurkhas, for example!

One great initiative that he took in 1990 was to look at the poor recruitment and retention of black and ethnic minority officers (a problem that I had looked at fifteen years before when I was at Management Services). He organised a two-day seminar in a college in Bristol for the fewer than 200 serving officers from BAME backgrounds so that their experiences could be compared and analysed to develop some positive recommendations for change. For all of us who took part and heard the accounts of petty bullying and bias at the hands of other officers, it was a searing and painful experience.

For them it was to be a rewarding experience, as for the first time they felt that their systemic problems were recognised; being thinly spread throughout London, they had often felt isolated and therefore reluctant to complain. It echoed my feelings of alienation at Battersea a decade earlier. They had already faced suspicion in their own communities for going over to 'the enemy', and were then met with discrimination within the police service. They were divided into groups, each with a facilitator. The accounts they gave of their treatment by other officers, including having their uniforms deliberately thrown on the floor, being excluded from social events and the persistent use of derogatory nicknames such as 'Paki', were heart-rending. None of us had realised how widespread their ill-usage (often justified as 'teasing') had been. There were two positive outcomes: one was the development of informal supportive networks and friendships, and the other was the formal establishment and recognition of the Black Officers Association to represent them.

After I had spent eight months of 1990 as Acting DAC, Ted Mitchell was due to return. I decided that although I could have served another two years, to the age of fifty-seven, the time had come to retire. There was a flurry of media interest in my retirement, so I had a half-page profile in the *Observer* with a rather disappointing photograph by that brilliant photographer Jane Bown. During the interview I made disparaging remarks about Margaret Thatcher's views on society and the denigration of public services, showing clearly where my political sympathies lay. I also appeared on *Start the Week* with Melvyn Bragg, but as Salman Rushdie was also on the programme I made little impact! It was, however, encouraging to have his security officers nodding in agreement at what I said about the importance of police officers being seen as part of society and not the tool of government.

24

RETIREMENT

The first few months of my retirement in the autumn of 1990 were a curious mixture of elation and despair. After a farewell party and generous leaving presents – the two-volume Shorter Oxford English Dictionary and a garden bench built by Harry Ball, my driver – I spent the last three weeks of my service on holiday in Rajasthan with Pauline. This was very different from my previous two trips to the north and south of India, and I have strong memories of it: the yellow sandstone towers of Jaisalmer rising like a mirage from the semi-desert where we were greeted by a small girl playing 'Over the Hills and Far Away' on a flute; the camel market where we slept in tents and stayed in the cool of an orchard during the day; the decaying Maharajah's palace where we slept in a half-furnished room with iron bedsteads and where there were bats in the bathroom and a hornet's nest on the balcony. All through the holiday, however, I was haunted by the fact that my sister Dinah's breast cancer had returned. Although a non-believer, I found myself saying prayers, subjecting myself to a *puja* with two opportunistic little boys by a sacred lake, and lighting votive candles.

The next few months were largely consumed by coping with Dinah's illness. I saw her practically every day, and while she was still at home in her flat helped with practicalities like paying bills. We had never been particularly affectionate before (the usual sibling rivalry) but became much closer at this time. When she was finally admitted to the Royal Free Hospital, I spent hours by her bedside doing tapestries while she dozed under the influence of the morphine pump. I think perhaps my worst Christmas ever was shopping for the necessary supplies of food, driving down to Wiltshire to our parents, cooking a Christmas dinner and returning to London after Boxing Day. Dinah refused to believe that she was dying, but in a brave spell of lucidity two weeks before her death she rang our parents to say goodbye and I wrote out her will for her (finding witnesses in the hospital was a problem as the nurses felt unable to sign) and a list of bequests. She said she wanted 'To Be a Pilgrim' to be sung at her funeral. She also said she wanted her ashes scattered on Grimms Dyke, where we had walked as children, and snowdrops to be planted there. My mother had sent up a box of snowdrops from the garden at Lacock. After that Dinah went into denial again. The hospital said that I should be finding a hospice for her, so, much against her wishes, I visited one where they were so sympathetic I burst into tears. However, she died the day before she was due to be moved.

Two days before she died in February 1991 there was a heavy snowstorm – no trains were running and a foot of snow made it impossible to drive. I felt desperate. However, it melted overnight and I spent her last day with her. Her friends Tasha and Tessa were also there (they had been stalwart and regular visitors) and, rather oddly, an old boyfriend, whom Tessa had traced. Being a Christian believer, he did provide comforting words about an afterlife. Her current boyfriend, a retired judge, was bewildered by this other man turning up and was taken down to the hospital canteen by Tessa and Tasha to keep him out of the way. I spent the day in a corner, compulsively playing patience with an old pack of cards, and was eventually comforted by the kindly presence of Pauline, who drove up from Bristol. Dinah died early the following morning, with Pauline and I holding her hands. We then went for a walk on Hampstead Heath, where I cried uncontrollably. I carried out her final wishes, arranged a rather bleak funeral which my father attended and subsequently went down to Berkshire with Pauline to scatter her ashes on Grimms Dyke and plant some snowdrops there.

I was frightened of retirement as I was not sure how I would cope without the familiar structure of the police service about me. The inscription that I had had put on the garden bench was from Voltaire. When Candide retires from public life, he says, '*Il faut cultiver notre jardin*' and this ironically was my expectation of retirement – that I would live in the country, have a large garden and perhaps get involved in local politics. However, the publicity I had when I left the police service had brought me to the attention of the Labour Party.

I was invited to tea by Tess, Lady Rothschild, whom I knew because we had been joint governors of our old school, Bedales. I had spent eight happy years in the 1980s as a Bedales governor in the company of not only Tess but also Charles Wheeler, the distinguished television reporter, and Dick White, the ex-head of MI6, who had of course known my father.

Tess asked me if I could live on my police pension if I were appointed to the House of Lords or whether I needed another job – the daily expense allowance in the Lords in those days was only £30. (It is now £300 for a full day or £150 for a half-day, but there is no longer an overnight allowance for those who live outside London.) I said to Tess that I could manage on my police pension as I had wholly paid off my mortgage.

I was then invited to meet Neil Kinnock, which I imagined would be a job interview but turned out to be a brief welcome to the fold provided I had not donated more than £20,000 to the Labour Party! I was able to reassure them on that point. I was then sworn to secrecy until there was a formal announcement later in the spring. My great sadness is that I was unable to tell Dinah, who would have so much enjoyed visiting me in the Lords and all the flummery.

My house had been on the market for some months in anticipation of leaving London – it was a rare moment of glut in the housing market, and I did not have central heating (since installed), so I was fortunately unable to sell and decided to stay in London. I had planned to live with Pauline in my retirement. We have remained friends, and I go to stay twice a year, but she now has other priorities. She also kindly fields Susie's daily telephone calls when I am abroad.

Distracted as I was by Dinah's illness, I had little time in January and February 1991 to think about the House of Lords – it just seemed a distant and agreeable prospect. I did not feel daunted as I imagined I had faced far worse ordeals in the police service.

I had only the faintest idea about how parliamentary business was conducted before my arrival, but I looked forward to working in that extraordinary building, which is such a confection of Pugin's Gothic, with gilding and linen-fold panelling everywhere, combined with high Victorian romanticism in the paintings of chivalric virtues and woodcuts of the Arthurian legend.

I enjoyed it all very much until I went to an exhibition of Pugin's work and was exhausted by all his Gothic houses and churches. On my first day in the Lords in May 1991 I had a miniature press conference at which a journalist asked, 'How will you cope with all those old male peers?' I said, 'Well, I have not been daunted by numerous chief constables, so I think I will manage.'

25

HOUSE OF LORDS

A major ethos of Bedales is that every human being of whatever gender is of equal value and that academic skills are of no more importance than social, manual or artistic skills. The school also, with few exceptions, treated boys and girls alike and made friendships across gender boundaries inherently possible. Although I encountered sexist and racist attitudes in the police service, it is an organisation which generally judges people as individuals and attaches great weight to personal characteristics and temperament.

It is in the House of Lords that I have been most patronised or ignored, so it is a delight when I encounter a fellow peer who treats me as an equal. Many peers were of course educated at single-sex public schools like Eton and still seem to treat women as a strange, exotic species. Ex-MPs also often appear to be an exclusive male club whose members reminisce nostalgically about life in the Commons. These are of course generalisations, and unfair to the many men in the Lords who treat women as equals.

My formal introduction (the only occasion apart from state openings when we wear robes) was preceded by a lunch with various friends and relatives including my father (my mother was unable to travel) who I am glad to say enjoyed all the flummery. Garter King at Arms (who always gets a free lunch on these occasions) was also present, dressed in a tabard like the white rabbit in *Alice in Wonderland*. Pauline and my irreverent friend Sonja giggled in the gallery above when I was taking the oath of allegiance to the Queen.

I had had a previous meeting with Garter King at Arms at the College of Heralds, who are responsible for titles and heraldic emblems, when I had to choose my title. All of the 'Garters' in my time in the Lords have been indistinguishable – ex-military men, stout and florid of face. Because my surname, Hilton, is a common name I was required to add a territory to distinguish it from other Hiltons. Having led a very peripatetic life, no particular location seemed obvious. In the end I settled on Eggardon, a hill in Dorset, now a National Trust site, where we used to have picnics and my grandmother sketched while I wandered on the ancient British earthworks. It has wonderful views over the Jurassic Coast and short-cropped grass. Garter said the title had to be a parish (only earls and dukes can have cities); fortunately it turned out to be on his list, although I know of no church there.

While with him I also discussed a design for a coat of arms. When Dinah died she left me £2,000, and I thought it might amuse my family to spend it on something as frivolous and useless as some heraldic emblems. Garter, who was not amused, thought it should be all about the police service, with handcuffs and crossed truncheons in blue and white. I, however, wanted references to school, family and university, and have ended up with a lovely bit of nonsensical artwork with only one small truncheon in sight clutched by one of the supporting beasts.

Otherwise it has roses for both Bedales and the Police College, a small snake for Manchester University and a tree on a small green hill surrounded by a fence to symbolise my concern for the environment.

My mentor and quasi-aunt, Nora, Baroness David (her husband's sister Ruth was married to my uncle Roger), said I should make my maiden speech as soon as possible, so in July I took part in a suppertime debate on adult education and talked about my experience and that of other police officers with inadequate educational backgrounds of the importance of being able to widen their horizons by attending evening classes and other courses. This was a time under the Tory government when the costs of evening classes were no longer to be heavily subsidised. As it was a suppertime debate I only had an audience of about thirty fellow peers so it was not too nerve-racking and I had several little congratulatory notes afterwards. One of the great pleasures of the Lords is the tendency to praise rather than criticise – very different from the police service.

Although loyal to the Labour Party as Neil Kinnock had appointed me, I am not as tribal as many of my colleagues who have been active in politics all their working lives, so I have friends in all parts of the House.

I have taken part in several legislative battles, and because of my police experience my first few years were largely spent attempting to ameliorate the worst ambitions of the Home Office to convert the police (and other public services) to a business model with a grossly flattened hierarchy. Our assault on this concept was ably led by John Harris, the Liberal peer, and we enlisted the support of the cross-bench ex-Chiefs of Staff of the Armed Services who understood the necessity of an adequate chain of command in operational situations. Our combined efforts met with some success and we retained the rank of chief inspector.

I was also present throughout the long battle to banish the 700 hereditary peers from the House. After long and wearisome sittings, many of them into the small hours of the night, a messy compromise was agreed that means we still have ninety-two hereditary peers (10 per cent of the total plus some office-holders) who are replaced when they die by means of ridiculous by-elections.

Subsequently, as my knowledge of the police service has become out of date, I have made speeches on a variety of subjects, mostly arising out of committee work, including when I chaired a small group looking at standards of behaviour in the House – a chronic concern which has been exacerbated by the unwanted increase in our numbers (notably by David Cameron) and the misbehaviour of a few members.

I made a major speech in 2002 opposing joining the United States in attacking Iraq (see Appendix 4). This, twelve months before the 2003 invasion, was a contribution to a splendid debate in the Lords with almost everyone including the ex-Chiefs of Staff, senior civil servants and politicians from all sides of the House, against this insane adventurism. I was briefly on the Foreign Affairs Committee that year and we went to Washington a month before the invasion and were horrified by the attitudes of the Senate, Pentagon and the right-wing Heritage Foundation NGO. Clearly no planning had gone into the aftermath of the invasion, and the Heritage Foundation accused us of being wimps with 'no experience of terrorism'. Our chairman, Lord Jopling, made an angry but measured response, pointing out that our country had been subjected to an IRA bombing campaign for many years but to little effect.

By this time I and others had spoken to Prime Minister Tony Blair, Foreign Secretary Jack Straw and Defence Secretary Geoff Hoon about our opposition. Their reactions to me were variously, mildly patronising, reasoning and indignantly hostile. At a reception in Downing Street I said to Tony Blair, 'I am one of your problems as I am totally opposed to the war on Iraq.' He smiled and said kindly but patronisingly, 'Only a small problem, Jenny.' Subsequently I joined in one of the public marches and made a mini-protest by not supporting government business for the next twelve months. Others – among them Philip Hunt, who was a Junior Minister of Health – made more principled stands, resigning their positions and salaries as ministers.

More recently I took part in a battle with the Tory government over the appointment of elected Police and Crime Commissioners to oversee the work of chief constables. This time the model was not the business world but the American system of having elected police chiefs. This might be appropriate in a small town, and is allegedly more democratic than having a police authority made up of local councillors, but does not make sense when one individual is supposed to represent a police force area that stretches across several counties. It is also very expensive as it requires premises and salaried staff.

I share an office with nine other peers but I am often alone as I open letters, reply to invitations and read the mass of evidence, lobbying letters, emails and periodicals that arrive each day. I have had the great privilege of sharing the office with great men such as Ralf Dahrendorf, who treated my naïve comments on nation states with apparent respect. I have also become very fond of John, the Earl of Selborne, erstwhile Chairman of Kew, who I persuaded to become the president of the charity of which I am a trustee, Life in Fresh Waters. We are a curious office – at one time, chairmen of committees had no designated desks so were allotted desks in this room, which is on the first floor on the west front, looking out at the apse of Westminster Abbey. As a result, we come from all three political parties and include a number of cross-benchers such as David Ramsbotham, ex-HM Chief Inspector of Prisons, and Alec Broers, an Australian engineer with a passion for ocean sailing who was Vice-Chancellor of Cambridge University.

Of course we have no secretarial support, but we are provided with an iPad or computer terminal on which to conduct all our correspondence. Despite this office work, my daily expenses require me to appear in the Lords Chamber to be ticked off on a list by one of the attendants. Sometimes if there is no whipped business requiring me to remain I go home after question time and only claim half expenses.

I usually go for an early lunch to the long table in the Peers' Dining Room (decorated with one of Pugin's less successful wallpapers in a bilious yellow). We sit in order of arrival, so I sometimes find myself with unexpected lunchtime companions. For many years I sat opposite Baroness Trumpington, who was also an early luncher. She was stimulating company but could be appallingly rude and disdainful. I soon learnt when not to pursue an argument! She was very proud of being an honorary lady-in-waiting to the Queen, which meant that she was often sent to Heathrow to greet foreign dignitaries. Despite her autocratic manners she was the only peer regularly invited to the staff Christmas parties. She became increasingly blind, and I often had to read the lunch menu to her. The same was true of Barbara Castle, famous when Minister of Transport for introducing the breathalyser and, against considerable opposition, the Equal Pay Act. She was lively, still flirtatious and always wore impeccable makeup. She confided one day that one of her assistants had to apply her lipstick and eyebrow pencil as she could no longer see to do it.

As I described earlier, on one occasion I found myself sitting next to Lord Longford who had just been to prison to visit Myra Hindley, the notorious child killer. He thought she should be released on parole, and when I disagreed with him he told me that I lacked compassion and that he would pray for me.

It is in the work of various committees that I have made my major contributions, and this is the work I particularly enjoy, because the committees are non-partisan and our recommendations to the government are dependent on the evidence brought before us. Committees usually meet once a week to hear evidence and there is a lot of written evidence to read between each meeting. I have been a member and chairman of the European Scrutiny Committee on the Environment. The six European Committees in the Lords have for many years scrutinised draft European directives and made recommendations for their improvement.

During my time on the committee, I briefly became an expert on bathing and drinking water, air quality, waste disposal, and recycling. Initially it was under the chairmanship of Jack Lewis, a distinguished Professor of Chemistry at Cambridge, who never made me feel uncomfortable about my lack of scientific knowledge. This committee also delightfully gave opportunities for foreign travel (although we did look at waste disposal sites in Sussex and Dundee as well) – usually to Brussels, but also further afield.

My most memorable trip abroad with Jack Lewis was to eastern Europe, to countries that were hoping to join the EU, to examine how European funds were being spent to help them bring their environments up to the required standards. Much of the money seemed to be being spent on western consultants, but we met some impressive local people. The Polish voivode responsible for the coal mining area around Krakow was an engineer who had worked all over the world and had a good understanding of the problems caused by his sulphurous coal. Across the Czech border, in another part of the 'Black Triangle', we visited a mayor who denied that there was any problem of air pollution even though his town was surrounded by dead and dying pine trees.

In Romania, the mayor of Ploesti in the oilfields just north of Bucharest had taught himself excellent English from the BBC World Service but presided over a desperate situation. The area is dotted with nodding donkeys and the oil refinery leaks so badly that the ground is saturated with oil. The local people were digging pits (smoking all the while) and scooping up oil in buckets. The fields seemed to be full of diseased and dying sheep, and when we visited the sewage works there was a film of oil on the surface of the sewage. Instead of reporting this problem, the works had devised a system of skimming off the oil and returning it to the refinery. It was my first experience of a totally command economy and a populace afraid of reporting to a higher authority. We also (as on later occasions) visited Ceausescu's monstrous palace. As an example of the callousness of his family, we were told that when they ran out of marble cladding for the walls his daughter went around the villages demanding that people give up their family tombstones.

Subsequently, when I was chairing the committee, we conducted a similar exercise in the Ukraine and Russia. Again, most of the European money was being spent on western consultants and there were insufficient staff in the European Commission to supervise projects. Some initiatives had borne fruit. The young man running the waterworks in St Petersburg (where they have an endemic problem with waterborne parasites to which the local population, but not tourists, are immune) had been on a three-month secondment to the River Trent Water Authority and was efficient and forward-looking. In Moscow, however, there were thunderstorms and it was difficult to keep awake whilst we listened to monologues by party apparatchiks who allowed no time for questions.

Probably my most enjoyable committee work has been as a member – and, for the last three years, chairman – of the Works of Art Committee, which buys and commissions paintings for the House. We had a tiny budget of £18,000 a year (which I helped enhance), but had fun commissioning works by students and unknown artists. We were also fortunate to have occasional donations of paintings or sculpture. A major task each year was to choose the Christmas cards for the House. This always caused trouble! Either people did not like our choice or the envelopes would not stick or they were too heavy for overseas mail. It was one of the tasks I was glad to relinquish when I was recycled off the committee. The normal tenure on a committee is three years, so I had been fortunate to have longer than that. One major success of my time on the committee was to increase the number of portraits of women on our walls, so that paintings of Shirley Williams, Valerie Amos (the first black Leader of the House of Lords) and Helene Hayman (the first woman Speaker of the House of Lords) now hang in the corridors and dining room.

Another of the most interesting and enjoyable aspects of my time in the Lords has been to act as an election monitor in the countries that were once part of the Soviet Union. About twenty years ago I was invited by our much-loved Chief Whip, Dennis Carter, to be Labour's representative on the OSCE (the Organisation for Security and Co-operation in Europe). This was set up after the collapse of the Soviet Union and includes Russia, the United States and fifty-five other countries. The headquarters are in Vienna, from where they coordinate work in all the old Soviet Republics to improve democratisation. The Parliamentary Association meets twice a year, once in Vienna and once in the summer in another capital. It is with this organisation that I have now monitored more than twenty elections.

My first experience of election monitoring was in Kyrgyzstan in January 1998. The weather was cold and clear, with a sprinkling of snow on the ground. At the polling station where we observed the opening there was a choir of large Russian women clothed in red and all seemingly six feet tall who sang songs (as our interpreter told us) about beautiful Kyrgyzstan. We had difficulty escaping from their imposing presence as they kept insisting we must listen to another song. Later that day, in tiny rural villages, it was clear that an election was a novelty as we had an audience of men in tall fur hats watching their fellow villagers cast their votes. At each polling station there were local women in bright yellow waistcoats who had been trained as civilian observers by the OSCE.

I seemed to specialise for some years in the Caucasus region – three elections each in Georgia, Armenia and Azerbaijan.

Armenia was memorable for the hospitality of local people, who invited us into their homes for coffee and delicious cherry jam. A dentist gave me a fossil from Mount Ararat (which hovers beautiful and snow-bound across the border in Turkey). A farmer's wife gave us tea and refused to believe my age, pulling up my trouser leg to inspect my ankles.

Most of these countries now run efficient and reasonably transparent elections. The exception is Azerbaijan, which continues to switch ballot boxes and falsify results. On one occasion in the foothills of the Caucasus we visited a polling station where as we arrived the chairman was stuffing bits of ballot papers into his pockets and a member of his committee had resigned in a fury. Some people had allegedly voted twice and the exit poll was being conducted inside the polling station so that people, having cast their votes in secret, were asked publicly how they had voted.

I have now visited the Ukraine many times for elections and conferences, and have enjoyed the opportunity in Kiev to visit the great monastic community of the Lavra, where there is an underground chapel with dark, narrow corridors lit only by candlelight and with the mummified corpses of previous abbots lying in niches. I love the early medieval church (deconsecrated by the Russians) of St Sophia, with its painted walls and the marble tomb of the tenth-century Yaroslav the Wise. On other occasions I have been to Odessa with its famous steps and to Dnipropetrovsk in the now war-torn east of the country.

One of the delights of the House of Lords has been the company of many distinguished people. Some of my early conversations, when we still had 700 hereditary peers, were disconcerting. It was difficult to join discussions about a weekend bag of grouse, and when talking about my garden pond one day I found that I was talking to a peer with a five-acre lake. These yawning gaps in lifestyle have not completely gone away – travelling up in the lift with Baroness Noakes recently, I said, 'It's nice to have some rain for the garden.' She replied, 'Yes, my horse likes soft running!'

It has, however, been a great privilege to be able to discuss *In Our Time* with Melvyn Bragg and he has been kind enough to take my comments seriously. We have had thriller writers like P. D. James and Ruth Rendell, distinguished lawyers, doctors like Robert Winston, and scientists and publishers (mostly on the Labour benches) who bring a wealth of knowledge from the world outside politics, and some like Joan Bakewell, with a willingness to address uncomfortable topics like old age and assisted dying. Alf Dubbs, who has become a dear friend, has shown extraordinary passion and commitment on behalf of refugee children and in campaigning against capital punishment all over the world. My other friend with whom I attend the twice-yearly OSCE conferences, Peter Bowness, is from the Tory benches; he has a genius for finding interesting lunch venues in various foreign cities.

Life outside the House of Lords has of course continued. I chaired the local amenity society for nine years and I do screen-printing once a week. Since my parents died twenty-five years ago I have become solely responsible for Susie. She lives in her own small terraced house near Chippenham. There have been some crises. She managed to set fire to her house when a neglected candle burnt down to the floorboards and spent some weeks in a local authority care home whilst it was restored. Then she spent one summer in a caravan on a caravan site near Malmesbury when her house had been condemned as unfit for human habitation and had to be cleaned and renovated. She now has daily visits from care assistants who keep her and her house reasonably clean and organised. They also take her out shopping and she buys innumerable flowering plants which then wither and die in her sitting room. I go down every two or three weeks and we have a pub lunch. In the spring and summer, we visit open gardens. I no longer have to worry so much about her, but it is still a relief to be able to escape to the House of Lords or on trips abroad.

Appendix 1

ORIGINS

This account of my ancestry did not fit comfortably into the narrative of my life but I think it is intrinsically interesting and is an important part of my sense of identity.

My mother was much more interested than my father in family history, so my information about her side of the family is more extensive. Her father, the barrister Pembroke Scott Stephens, had elaborate family trees drawn up and printed which when unrolled extended to about twelve feet. They showed ancestors which included a drover, a glover and a surgeon, Richard Denham, who served with Cromwell's brutal army in Ireland. They also had details of an eighteenth-century family called 'Unthank' who had twenty-three children, many of whom had no names but are shown by question marks – presumably because they died in infancy.

My Father's Ancestry

John Robert Hilton was born on 5 January 1908, and came on his mother's side from a long line of Derbyshire (Holdsworth) owners of land and coal mines (my father said, 'Derbyshire born and

Derbyshire bred, long in the arm and short in the head'; my mother snobbishly said, 'Good yeomen stock') and on his father's side he came from a family of German-Jewish jute merchants based in Hamburg. His father, Oscar Hildesheim, was the youngest of ten children and was born in Dundee where his father, David, was managing a branch of the family's jute business (Dundee was then famous for jam, jute and journalism). There was another branch of the family business in Sweden.

My father had a memorable summer holiday on a small Swedish island with his Swedish cousins and with a great-aunt, an expert on trilobites, who smoked cigars in bed. The mother of my grandfather, Oscar, my great-grandmother, was Suzette Warburg, sister to Abe Warburg, the founder of the Warburg Institute, so hers was a well-off and cultured family. Almost all the German members of the family, his cousins, with whom he had stayed in Hamburg as a young man, perished in the Holocaust. It was a topic he was never willing to discuss.

My grandfather, Oscar, was educated at Magdalen College, Oxford, and at St Thomas' Hospital in London and became a GP. He was always known as 'Papoose' to his grandchildren because he preferred to be called the Greek version when I was born in Cyprus rather than the English 'Grandpa'. Several of his brothers and sisters were artists and went to the Slade School of Art, where Louisa Holdsworth, my grandmother, and her sister Lila were studying and so Louisa and Oscar met and subsequently married. Louisa was devoutly Church of England but Oscar was a non-observant Jew. During the First World War, when my father was six, German names became so unpopular that Oscar changed his surname from Hildesheim to Hilton. (Confusingly, his brothers and sisters chose other surnames such as Hunt and Home.)

My father was so angry at this loss of identity that he scratched 'John Hildesheim' into the varnished top of the large dining room table. He was the oldest of four children. His brother Michael became the diplomatic correspondent of the *Daily Telegraph*, his brother Roger became a well-known abstract-expressionist artist, and his sister Judy became my lively and bossy godmother.

My Mother's Ancestry

My mother was born in 1909 on my father's first birthday – 5 January. Her ancestry was much more complicated, containing elements of Scottish Presbyterianism, Lithuanian musicianship, the Arts and Craft movement, and many Irish strands, largely in fact Scottish, such as Captain Scott from Orkney, and many with English names such as Warner, Denham and Swanzy, all of whom settled in Dublin. Some of these elements have an almost mythic quality, such as Edward Warner, who came from Sweden and was said to have tutored Queen Elizabeth I and Edward VI. On more solid ground is the story of descent from John Knox's brother William, since a great-grandmother was a Knox.

The Arts and Craft/William Morris connection is my great-grandfather Walter Townsend, whose brother Charles Harrison Townsend was the architect of many houses and churches in a vaguely Byzantine style but also of the Whitechapel Art Gallery, the Bishopsgate Institute and the Horniman Museum – all in furtherance of William Morris's vision that art and culture should be available to everyone. He also painted exquisite small watercolour Swiss landscapes, some of which I have, and designed patterns for woven cloths and fantasy alphabets.

The Townsends were also very proud of their descent from a distinguished Lithuanian musician, the violinist Felix Yanovitch or Yaniewicz or Janiewicz, who was born in 1762 in Vilnius when Lithuania was united with Poland under a single royal family. The family myth is that he was an illegitimate child of the Lithuanian monarchy, or possibly Jewish. My mother tried to establish the truth of his origins through a researcher in Vilnius but the disruptions of the past two centuries have left little in the way of records. The facts that are known are that in the 1780s he was sent by King Stanislas to Vienna where he studied with Mozart and Haydn. Haydn wrote a piece for him to play on his violin. He was later in Paris, but the French Revolution was in full swing and his home country was in total disarray and under the heel of Russia, so in 1792 he came to London and played in many concerts including benefit concerts for Haydn and Pleyel. He also played one of his own concertos with Pleyel at the piano. He seems to have been a prolific composer as well as a gifted violinist and a partner in a piano-making business in Liverpool.

In 1800, Felix Yanovich married a Miss Eliza Breeze in Liverpool and they subsequently moved to Edinburgh, where they settled and he established an annual music festival (that may have been a precursor of the Edinburgh Festival). There is an engraved inscription in Edinburgh New Town on the stone frontage of one of those imposing houses in which the family lived. There were two daughters, Pauline and Felicia. One of the stories about Felix (never to be mentioned according to his wife) is that early in the nineteenth century a group of Lithuanians came to see him (wearing fur hats and with snow on their boots) to persuade him to take the throne in Lithuania. The only corroboration of this story is that his personal crest on his silverware was a mailed arm holding a sword with the motto 'Pro Lithuania' beneath. He died in 1848 at the age of eighty-six.

Felix's daughter Pauline (1808–1896) was also a professional violinist. She married a solicitor, Jackson Townsend (1804–1883), in Liverpool and they had four sons and two daughters. The sons all had to earn their own living, so whilst Charles Harrison Townsend became a distinguished architect, his younger brother by two years, Walter Mallaby Townsend (1848–1905), my great-grandfather, had to find employment abroad and went to Canada to work for the Canadian Pacific Railway Company. He had already met and married his formidable wife, St Clair Denham (1853–1935), born in Dublin, whose mother was a Knox given to charitable actions ('the Angel' of Mecklenburgh Square in Dublin) and whose father was an ambidextrous surgeon, John Denham, Master of the Rotunda in Dublin. Walter and St Clair had three daughters, of whom the eldest, Pauline (Pau-Pau), was my grandmother. The other two were St Clair (Saintie) and Helen.

My great-grandmother St Clair was always known as 'Bonnemaman'. On their return to England from Canada she ran a marble mine in Northumbria and became a town councillor in Northwood but surprisingly wrote an article denouncing the suffragettes' campaign! Poor Walter was ill suited to life as a businessman – he wrote plays and took part in amateur dramatics – so drowned his disappointments in alcohol. In 1898, at the age of twenty, my grandmother Pauline was married to a friend of the family, sixty-five-year-old Pembroke Scott Stephens (1834–1914). This marriage was probably arranged by 'Bonnemaman' with an eye to his wealth. She apparently greatly enjoyed spending money on furnishing both his houses – one in the Regent's Park terraces (where my mother was born) and the other Missenden House in Little Missenden, Buckinghamshire, where he owned most of the village (two farms and several houses).

Pembroke Scott Stephens was allegedly a virgin when he married (so my father said, although the source of his knowledge is unknown but possibly his mother-in-law, my grandmother) and was a very successful self-made man. He was a barrister at the Parliamentary Bar, a journalist and a deputy editor of *The Times*. He was born in Dublin in 1835 but his mother died when he was less than a year old and his father, who was a pharmacist and journalist, died in Portugal in 1844 so he was largely brought up by his grandmother and an aunt. His grandmother, born Eleanor Warner and once married to a Captain Scott from Orkney, was widowed in 1846 and remained a dominant influence in his life until her death in 1880 at the age of ninety-one.

These ill-assorted maternal grandparents of mine nevertheless had four children (two, Pat and Pauline, were twins), although my grandmother allegedly had a breakdown after each birth and went painting in France. She was an accomplished watercolourist and had also been to the Slade like my other grandmother, mother and uncle. Her eldest child, Philip, became a journalist with *The Telegraph* and was killed when observing a battle in the Sino-Japanese War in 1937. He was in a water tower with other journalists when it was apparently deliberately shelled by the Japanese, who disliked his comments about the atrocities they had committed in Nanking – it was a cause celebre at the time and occupied the whole front page of *The Telegraph*. Then there were the twins, Pauline and Pat, always held up as sporting and scholastic examples to my mother, who was the youngest and not at all sporty, although she was enthusiastic about riding, had her own horse, and rode to hounds. She was christened Margaret Frances but was always known as Peggy. Her father, Pembroke Stephens, died when she was six, and her mother, my grandmother, Pau-Pau, married her second husband, Harry Boucher, within a year; this apparently scandalized all of Little Missenden.

The consequence for my mother was that she was constantly sent away to a succession of boarding schools. She was happy at some – like Pinewood, a Quaker school run by Margery Fry – and less happy at others. At the bleak St Leonards, on the east coast of Scotland, she was cold and miserable, and stuck in the shadow of her twin sisters, who had excelled both athletically and scholastically at the school. It is perhaps symptomatic of her unhappy childhood that her fondest memories of home are of eating sausages and mash with the kitchen staff. Her mother was soon a widow once more and used my mother as a companion to travel around France and Austria, where there were picnics and swimming on the banks of the Danube with delightful Austrian friends. On one trip, Pau-Pau contracted typhoid and they spent six weeks together in lovely Dubrovnik.

On the strength of her languages, my mother was accepted by Somerville College, Oxford, but was unable to pass the Latin exams so left after two terms and went to the Slade School of Art (like her mother, future mother-in-law and future brother-in-law). It was there that she met up again with my father, who was studying architecture at the RIBA nearby. The families had known each other when my parents were children in Northwood, a suburb of north-west London, where my paternal grandfather, Oscar, was a GP and where Bonnemaman had also settled when she was widowed and became a town councillor (there is a road, ambiguously, named after her, 'Townsend' Road). Her brother-in-law, the architect Charles Harrison Townsend, a lifelong bachelor, also lived in Northwood, as did his sister Lina.

My father's education was much more straightforward than my mother's. He spent a term at Rugby before moving to Marlborough, on a scholarship each time. He was very homesick to begin with and wrote heartbreaking letters home, but he eventually settled down and made friends, specifically with the poet Louis MacNeice and Anthony Blunt, later Keeper of the Queen's Pictures and subsequently unmasked as a spy, to my father's astonishment. The three boys saw themselves as aesthetes opposed to the rugger hearties and wrote poetry together. It was perhaps fortunate for many reasons that Anthony Blunt went to Cambridge whilst my father went to Oxford, but they did have a holiday together as students visiting Baroque churches in Germany and sleeping in ditches. Anthony was an inattentive godfather to one of my sisters and was disliked by my mother.

The only sport that my father enjoyed at school was cross-country running, although he rowed for his college at Oxford in the 'Bump' races and later was enthusiastic about scrambling on rocks. At Oxford he initially read mathematics but then switched to PPE (philosophy, politics and economics). Philosophy became a lifelong hobby and he was a member of the Aristotelian Society and regularly corresponded with Isaiah Berlin. On leaving Oxford he felt he should do 'something useful' and studied to become an architect (he would, I think, have been much more suited to an academic and professorial life – indeed, encouraged by Louis MacNeice he did, unsuccessfully, apply for a lectureship at Birmingham University). It was because he was an architect that he was selected by the Cyprus Committee to prop up their crumbling ancient monuments and why I was born there.

After leaving the Slade in the early 1930s, my mother went to live in Paris and studied in the atelier of the French artist Bissière.

My father's brother Roger was also there and they seem to have led a rather rackety life, with Roger having various love affairs, possibly with my mother and almost certainly with my mother's French friend Guilhen, of whom he painted several portraits (one of which I have). My mother lodged with Guilhen's family, the Perriers, and Guilhen became my mother's lifelong friend with whom I stayed many times. She married Daniel Douady, a distinguished doctor, and they had five children, both older and younger than me, and I thought of them as my second family.

My father seems to have become worried at this point about Roger's attentions to my mother, so, having finally qualified as an architect, he formally proposed to her and was accepted. They were married on 3 September 1933 at Marylebone Registry Office.

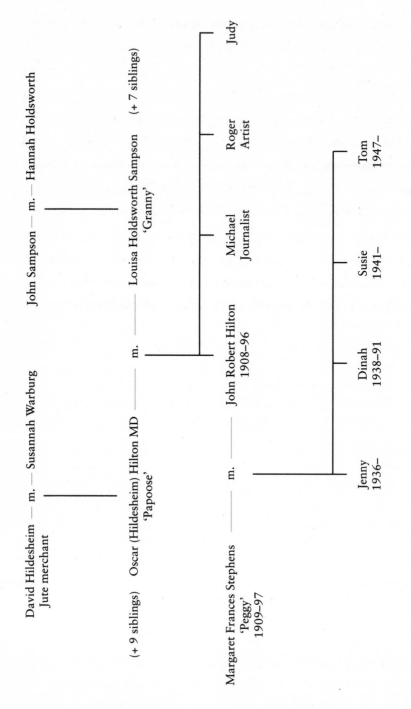

David Hildesheim — m. — Susannah Warburg
Jute merchant

John Sampson — m. — Hannah Holdsworth

(+ 9 siblings)   Oscar (Hildesheim) Hilton MD ——— m. ——— Louisa Holdsworth Sampson   (+ 7 siblings)
                 'Papoose'   'Granny'

Margaret Frances Stephens ——— m. ——— John Robert Hilton
'Peggy'   1908–96
1909–97

Michael   Roger   Judy
Journalist   Artist

Jenny   Dinah   Susie   Tom
1936–   1938–91   1941–   1947–

My father's family tree

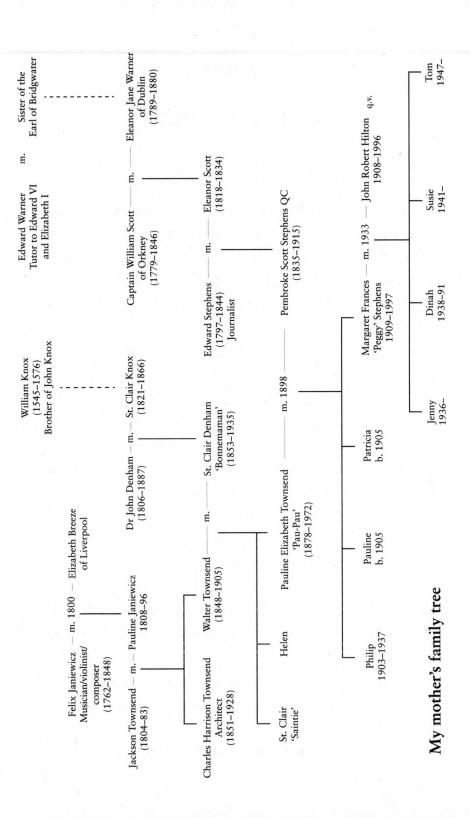

My mother's family tree

Appendix 4

SPEECH ON IRAQ

I made this speech in a debate initiated by Baroness Shirley Williams on 10 April 2002, nearly twelve months before the actual invasion, when almost all the House of Lords, including the ex-Chiefs of Defence, condemned the idea of attacking Iraq. Many of my predictions were not borne out by events but it did become a disaster in other ways.

My Lords, for more than a month I have been deeply concerned about President's Bush's statement that the next stage in the war against terrorism would be an attack on Iraq. I thought for some weeks that I was – Cassandra-like – a voice crying in the wilderness. The metaphors that spring to mind come appropriately from Greek tragedies and the Old Testament. But the chorus of disquiet about the dangers of sowing dragons' teeth is now widespread. I am grateful to the noble Baroness, Lady Williams, for the opportunity to express my disquiet.

The reality of what is happening in Israel is already having the consequences that would arise from attacking Iraq. As has already been said the moderate Arab states in the Middle East and North Africa are increasingly alienated. Sudan has already offered training camps for Palestinian terrorists and there have been attacks on synagogues in France. These consequences would be exacerbated by military action against Iraq. Terrorism would become more, not less, widespread.

Terrorism is a response to grievance where there are no alternative channels for protest. Of course Yasser Arafat's tragic endorsement of the young suicide bombers has been desperately provocative but their resort to terrorism is fuelled by underlying and genuine grievances. Israel's occupation of the West Bank and the illicit building of settlements should have been tackled by the international community, especially by the United States, a long time ago.

President Bush is allegedly surprised by the antagonism of the surrounding Arab states to Israel's behaviour. I hope that he will now begin to understand the likely consequences of an attack on Iraq. The various military scenarios that have been promulgated include 10,000 civilian casualties and possibly the need for an invasion force of 250,000 military personnel with many more dead on both sides. Iraq is not Afghanistan. Saddam Hussein has 350,000 troops and a military conflict on that scale would effectively amount to a third world war as other states were drawn in.

Much as the governments of the moderate Arab states may dislike Iraq, many of their young people in countries as widespread as Morocco, Egypt, Saudi Arabia, Pakistan and Indonesia, see Osama bin Laden and Saddam Hussein as heroes because they stand up to the might of the United States. The disaffected youth of many of those countries are posing an increasing problem because of their numbers. Forty per cent of Morocco's population of 45 million are aged under 18. Of Saudi Arabia's population of 23 million, forty three per cent are under 15. There are in consequence increasing numbers of unemployed youths to whom terrorism may seem like an attractive alternative career which would be justified by an American attack on Iraq. Saudi Arabia has 100,000 young people coming into the job market each year of whom only half find jobs.

Terrorism is a hydra-headed monster – the more heads you cut off, the more will grow in their place. Terrorism is easily exported as America knows to its cost. As the French learnt in Algeria and we learnt in Northern Ireland, military measures may contain the problem in the short term, but are no long-term solution.

A worrying aspect about both Ariel Sharon and George Bush is that their actions appear to be dictated by a sense of unfinished business. For the United States to be so indignant about a country's failure to comply with the United Nation's resolutions comes uncomfortably from a country that has not enforced UN resolutions on Israel, that has failed to pay its UN dues on occasion, that breaks international treaties on trade and arms without compunction, and that declines to take part with the international community in combatting global warming and the setting up of the International Criminal Court.

If the United States' argument that a pre-emptive attack on Iraq is legitimised by self-defence, why not attack North Korea which is an equally repressive regime and which has nuclear weapons and missiles that could reach the western seaboard of the United States?

I hope that when the Minister replies she will confirm that no military attack is intended to change the regime in Iraq without an explicit resolution from the United Nations. Moreover, I do not accept that failure to conform to previous resolutions or the vague necessity of self-defence are sufficient justification for launching what would effectively be a third world war.

Appendix 5

SPEECH ON INTERNATIONAL AFFAIRS

My Lords,

It has been a privilege to be a member of a Committee chaired by Lord Howell and containing several other distinguished members of your Lordships' House. It is a great regret to me that I shall be 'recycled' at the end of June.

Our report, as has already been said, had two main themes. Firstly, an examination of the shifting power balances in the world and the breakdown of a rule-based order for trade and diplomatic relations. I am however doubtful that such an order ever existed. It was rather that the dominance of the United States made it seem that there was a worldwide consensus on how to conduct international relations. China, Russia and many developing nations have been outside the club and played by different rules.

Our second theme was the rise of new technology with its instant means of communication and provision of intelligence. Traditional forms of diplomacy often depended on personal and confidential relationships that allowed negotiations to take place behind closed doors and could ignore uncomfortable realities. It is no longer possible to ignore China's treatment of the Uighurs in Xinjiang Province when aerial photographs show the vast internment camps and the destruction of ancient mosques.

Rapid responses are therefore now required to unfolding events. In the nineteenth century it took 3 months to assemble an army in response to the tragedy of the 'Indian Mutiny', but in a time of instant information flow it becomes all the more important to have well-thought-out and long-term strategies so that short-term tactical responses can fall within an established strategic framework.

China has unfair trade practices but it does take a long-term view and pursues collaboration with other countries. Their belt and road policy, which may still have more illusion than reality, has provided much-needed infrastructure for developing countries, although often placing them under an unsupportable level of debt. It is also providing the groundwork for extensive trading opportunities. My Lords, China is changing so fast. When I first visited Shanghai nearly 40 years ago it was dingy and down at heel and our hotel had the largest cockroaches I have ever seen. Now it is a shining city of high-rise blocks and has perhaps the largest port for container ships in the world.

Much more worrying is the destabilising role of the United States which even without the antics of their President is becoming ever more isolationist and protectionist. Contrary to the assumption that we have a 'Special Relationship' with the United States we see an ever-widening gulf of attitudes and behaviour. Their denigration of the United Nations and reluctance to join in any international agreements is deeply disturbing. There is a long list of undermining any international consensus or treaty.

These include withdrawal from the Convention on Climate Change, the Iran Deal, and most recently, from a global deal to cut plastic waste sponsored by the United Nations. They are also limiting the scope of the World Trade Organisation by failing to appoint members to the dispute resolution board so woe betide us if we end up subject to WTO rules. They are obsessive about forcing Iran into submission whilst happily trading with Saudi Arabia which has an even worse human rights record. At least in Iran women can drive cars and there are elections!

The UK's response to the worsening in international relations will depend in part on working with other like-minded countries (and we are about to cut ourselves off from the largest bloc of such nations). We do still by ourselves have some influence in the world despite our current chaotic politics. Our trade deals can be made to be free of bribery and other kickbacks and can ensure that they do not discriminate against women or ethnic minorities. In respect of climate change, however, we have not been an ideal role model. We have reduced subsidies on solar power generation – incidentally putting several small firms of installers out of business. We are allowing fracking and prohibiting onshore wind farms.

Now that the crisis is more generally recognised I hope, as recently promised by a government minister, that we will aim to lead the world and be carbon neutral by 2050. Also, as our reliance on hydrocarbons diminishes and we increase our usage of renewable sources of energy, we may be able to rethink our relationship with countries such as Saudi Arabia.

There are other ways of showing leadership and demonstrating our values to the world. Symbolism is important. The fact that two of our embassies flew LGBT flags on 17 May – the World's International Day Against Homophobia – was a valuable demonstration and gave comfort and encouragement to local activists. This display of tolerance and non-discrimination is in stark contrast to the activities of American evangelical Christians who have been active in countries such as Uganda promoting hatred and bigotry.

Overall, My Lords, I am making a plea for a long-term strategic approach to current affairs, working in concert with other countries so that our reaction to events is not erratic and arbitrary and the world becomes a safer and more stable place where we can work together to deal with the greatest threat of all, which is Climate Change.